Palgrave Studies in Global Citizenship Education and Democracy

Jason Laker
San Jose State University,
California, USA

This series will engage with the theoretical and practical debates regarding citizenship, human rights education, social inclusion, and individual and group identities as they relate to the role of higher and adult education on an international scale. Books in the series will consider hopeful possibilities for the capacity of higher and adult education to enable citizenship, human rights, democracy and the common good, including emerging research and interesting and effective practices. It will also participate in and stimulate deliberation and debate about the constraints, barriers and sources and forms of resistance to realizing the promise of egalitarian Civil Societies. The series will facilitate continued conversation on policy and politics, curriculum and pedagogy, review and reform, and provide a comparative overview of the different conceptions and approaches to citizenship education and democracy around the world.

More information about this series at
http://www.springer.com/series/14625

Kevin Smith

Curriculum, Culture and Citizenship Education in Wales

Investigations into the Curriculum Cymreig

Kevin Smith
Cardiff University
Cardiff, United Kingdom

Palgrave Studies in Global Citizenship Education and Democracy
ISBN 978-1-137-54442-1   ISBN 978-1-137-54443-8   (eBook)
DOI 10.1057/978-1-137-54443-8

Library of Congress Control Number: 2016939275

Printed on acid-free paper

This Palgrave Macmillan imprint is published by Springer Nature
The registered company is Macmillan Publishers Ltd. London.

Introduction

This book is the culmination of research conducted over a period of seven years. While each study is generally associated with citizenship education, collectively they are primarily concerned with how cultural identity, and, further to the point, Welshness is constructed, promoted, and evaluated through school curricula in Wales. While conversations of citizenship are typically concerned with issues of rights, responsibilities, and privileges, citizenship also has a psychological and sociological dimension in that it also involves constructions of self, other, and the performance of how we understand and respond to these socially constructed representations. The contents of this book take into consideration the definition and representation of Welshness through curricular guidance provided to teachers by the Welsh Government, students' definitions and descriptions of Welshness and what they think it means to be Welsh, pupils' perceptions of how schooling affects their orientations to, and affiliations with, Wales and Welshness, and teachers' perspectives on how citizenship education and cultural identity are currently taught in schools in Wales. Although the studies in this book were conducted separately, they each share common themes exploring the relationship between the people learning and teaching in schools in Wales, curriculum, and cultural identity.

In the autumn of 2008, I undertook an ethnographic project involving 65 Sixth Form students at secondary school in mid-Wales. Over the course of four months, I interviewed these students asking them questions about their schooling experience and its relationship to their understanding of culture, Wales, and Welshness. Their responses were candid and insightful and provided me with a perspective on how curriculum engages, or fails to engage, students in conversations of cultural identity and citizenship. This insight fuelled my interest in exploring the official curricular narratives that define cultural identity in Wales and the guidance provided for teachers in incorporating those narratives into the schooling experiences of their pupils and students. This new perspective, informed by the students' discussions of their schooling experiences, eventually led me to conduct a critical discourse analysis of *Developing the Curriculum Cymreig*, a Welsh Government policy document, in 2010. This document outlines the aims and goals of the Curriculum Cymreig and provides case studies representing best practices intended to inspire and instruct teachers in enacting a Curriculum Cymreig in their classroom practice. Although I do not include the findings from that analysis in this book, I have summarised them and refer to them often as they provide an important context for later developments in citizenship education curricula and cultural identity promotion in schools in Wales. In 2013, I was fortunate to begin working in Wales after two years as the Fellow in Curriculum at the University of the South Pacific in 'Atele, Tonga. After "coming home" to Wales (my mother was born in Wales and I have always had a strong connection to Wales and Welshness), I wanted to enhance my understanding of the potential impact of the Curriculum Cymreig on pupils. Through my work with WISERD (The Wales Institute for Social & Economic Research Data & Methods at Cardiff University) on the WISERD Education study, I initiated research focusing on the following questions derived from the aims and goals of the *Developing the Curriculum Cymreig* document: "Does schooling help you appreciate living in Wales?" and "does schooling help you develop your own sense of Welshness?" I was interested in knowing the pupils' perspective. Did they feel like their school and teachers were engaging them in appreciating the distinctiveness of life in Wales and their associations with Welshness? The findings of this research eventually led me to question teachers about how they teach citizenship and cultural identity to their pupils, and how they might envision new approaches to these subjects that might better inform pupils' and teachers' understanding and expectations of learning and living in Wales. In addition to teachers' discussions of Welshness and the Curriculum Cymreig, I also discuss approaches to citizenship education with Welsh Baccalaureate and Personal and Social Education (PSE) teachers regarding their experiences with teaching citizenship in Wales.

Citizenship is a vast concept open to a multiplicity of interpretations and representations. In this book, I focus most of my discussion on one of the key elements of citizenship education curricula in Wales—cultural identity—and how it is constructed and represented through curricular policy, promoted by teachers and their classroom practice and understood by young people attending schools in Wales. From these discussions, I offer recommendations for new approaches to thinking about cultural identity in Wales involving a critical approach to education that resists technical and instrumental approaches to teaching and learning about identity. Concerns over identity, representation, and performance are key elements to the field of critical pedagogy, and this particular framework for teaching and learning can provide a myriad of new approaches for teachers and young people to conceptualise and discuss Welshness, with the hope that through these approaches pupils and teachers can develop their critical literacy and recognise how certain assumptions about culture and identity are constructed and promoted through curricula. From the exercise of these skills, they can hopefully gain a better understanding of the importance of diversity, cultural identity, and the benefits of philosophically engaging in their education.

ACKNOWLEDGEMENTS

The information presented in this book is a culmination of research regarding the Curriculum Cymreig. My relationship with this interesting curricular initiative goes back to 2008 when I first learned of the curriculum and its goals and aims. Over the course of seven years, my interest in schooling in Wales continued, and time after time, I found myself returning to questions about the Curriculum Cymreig. Like all research endeavours, this book would not have been possible without the support and cooperation of many different people and organisations. In 2010, I completed my doctoral thesis, a critical discourse of *Developing the Curriculum Cymreig*, in the Department of Educational Leadership at Miami University in Oxford, Ohio. This analysis of the guidance for the Curriculum Cymreig has served as the foundation for much of my later research. In addition, I am particularly grateful for my involvement with the WISERD Education study, a longitudinal study funded by the Higher Education Funding Council for Wales (HEFCW) involving nearly 1500 pupils in over 30 schools. I would also like to thank the pupils, teachers, and parents involved in this research, as well as the many instructors, colleagues, friends, and mentors who have supported me in writing this book. Most important, I would like to especially thank my wife and children for their loving support and constant inspiration. Rwi'n dy garu di.

CONTENTS

LIST OF TABLES

CHAPTER 1

Citizenship Education in the UK

Abstract Smith introduces the origins of citizenship education (CE) in the UK and how concerns in the other home nations regarding young peoples' engagement with politics, community, and concepts of citizenship were interpreted through additional concerns over cultural and national identity in Wales. This, and the advent of devolution in Wales, eventually led to the development of a number of curricular interventions, including Personal and Social Education (PSE), school-level mandates for strategies addressing Education for Sustainable Development and Global Citizenship (ESDGC), and, perhaps the most distinctive policy accompanying the national curriculum for Wales, the Curriculum Cymreig.

Keywords Citizenship Education • Wales • Personal and Social Education • Education for Sustainable Development and Global Citizenship • Curriculum • Curriculum Cymreig

Citizenship, in all of its various forms and interpretations, has existed as a common concern throughout the history of schooling in the UK. This concern has been, and continues to be, mobilised through a number of political and ideological interpretations regarding the nature of citizenship and its role in society. Community engagement, civic action, social inclusion, and democratic participation are some of the expected outcomes of a schooling experience concerned with citizenship. However, until relatively

© The Editor(s) (if applicable) and The Author(s) 2016   1
K. Smith, *Curriculum, Culture and Citizenship Education in Wales*,
DOI 10.1057/978-1-137-54443-8_1

recently, specific curricular conversations for how these outcomes were to be produced were largely missing from educational policy and school management in the UK. In recent years, the lack of a coherent and purposeful approach to citizenship education (CE), coupled with a perceived disenfranchisement from electoral politics and community engagement among young people, has caused concern among politicians, policymakers, educators, and community stakeholders regarding the health of democracy in the UK, and by extension, the communities in which young people live and learn.

Additionally, the challenges posed to ethnically, culturally, and economically diverse communities (Stoker and Hay 2009; Kymlicka 1996; Mair 2008; Young 2002) have prompted educational policymakers and educators to develop a more concerted approach to educating for citizenship and ameliorating what some scholars (Marsh et al. 2007; Pattie et al. 2004; Sloam 2007) have described as the democratic disaffectedness experienced by so many in the UK. The political circumstances and social concerns that motivated the introduction of CE in the UK are discussed further on in this book. In this chapter, I focus on how CE is conceptualised and delivered in Wales.

CE IN WALES

In its earliest form, CE throughout the UK was implemented as a non-compulsory, cross-curricular theme (Daugherty and Jones 1999). However, it was later endorsed as a statutory subject in England in September 2002 (Watson 2004). In Wales, CE is not a stand-alone subject. Instead, it is delivered through Personal and Social Education (PSE), Education for Sustainable Development and Global Citizenship (ESDGC), and the Welsh Baccalaureate. Conceptually, CE is an attempt to help pupils develop political literacy—meaning that they are able to recognise, comprehend, and act on the characteristics of citizenship in their communities, the nation, and even on a global scale.

The introduction of CE in the UK comes from concerns over young peoples' attitudes towards civic and political participation and the desire to strengthen the public sphere by helping young people understand how political processes work and how to actively engage in those processes (Frazer 1999; Jowell and Park 1998). In the late 1990s, the Advisory Group on Citizenship was established and a report was commissioned to help clarify approaches to CE in school. The report claimed citizenship was more than a subject for learning. In fact, it was a concept that, if taught well and tailored to local needs, would enhance the democratic life of all people in society. In order for schools to be the hub for the development of practices of good citizenship, curricula needed to allow students to approach and meaningfully engage in the basic foundations of citizenship. From its inception, CE in England involved an understanding of people acting together to address issues of common concern. This concern and ability to engage in social and civic processes was believed to lead to a stronger democratic culture and a more inclusive society.

In Wales, the origins of citizenship remained squarely within a communitarian discourse framed within a desire to identify (or promote) a distinctive quality of associated living from that of (primarily) England and the other home nations. As concepts of citizenship in Wales continued to emerge in educational and political discourse, discourses of Welshness remained squarely fixed to concepts of citizenship.

The rhetoric supporting citizenship curricula in schools has typically framed citizenship in lofty terms that propose challenges to teachers who are working to meet the requirements of the curriculum in ways that could be incorporated into lessons, accessible by pupils, and accurately assessed and evaluated. For example, in England teachers were expected to create learning opportunities intended to allow pupils to explore questions about democracy, justice, inequality, and the processes of social governance and organisation. Guidance for teachers in England suggests learning experiences where pupils learn to work together to create solutions that try to address challenges facing their neighbourhoods and wider communities. As part of this process, teachers were also expected to assist their pupils in developing political literacy, which, in turn, will enable them as well-informed and "responsible" citizens to make positive contributions to society. While specific examples for how teachers were to accomplish these lofty goals were not specifically outlined by government guidance, foundations and support groups for CE began to pop up across the educational landscape.

As CE policy and curricula became more defined in England and elsewhere in the UK, Wales too, through its relatively newly devolved powers in education, began to develop its own distinctive approach. In terms of theoretical development, CE in Wales was organised and communicated through two key policies: "Community Understanding" and the "Curriculum Cymreig." In 1991, *Community and Understanding* was published by the Welsh Government. This document laid out a series of guidelines designed to provide a "complex, multi-faceted definition" of community (Phillips and Daugherty 2000, p. 93). The document claims that thoughtful approaches to understanding community will help pupils to "identify and appreciate the common experience of their cultural heritage as well as understand its diverse and distinctive aspects" (CCW 1991, p. 2). It further promoted the idea that understanding community in ways that address diversity, inequality, and prejudice is central to situating community within a discourse of Welshness—of Welsh culture, or Cymreig. Two years following this publication, the Welsh Government published *Developing the Curriculum Cymreig*, the official guidance for a curricular initiative that was intended to enable educators to incorporate themes of Welshness into their school ethos. More than simply teaching "Welshness," the Curriculum Cymreig operates as the primary organisational feature for how concepts of citizenship and cultural identity are to be promoted in schools in Wales. Since the early 1990s, this distinctive feature of the national curriculum has survived many changes in policy and personnel, and it continues to exist as a distinguishing feature from other national curricula in the UK.

Surprisingly, even with the popularity of CE in recent years, Wales continues to rely on the Curriculum Cymreig as the primary vehicle through which teachers and pupils come to think about models for associated living and cultural identity. While initiatives promoting sustainable development and global citizenship work in tandem with PSE lessons, the Curriculum Cymreig and the guidance supporting the initiative, remain as the overarching, theoretical framework informing how teachers and pupils interact with discussions of cultural identity. Due to the ubiquitous nature of the Curriculum Cymreig in Welsh schooling and its relationship to citizenship and identity, the primary focus of this book is to present research that engages the Curriculum Cymreig from the perspective of pupils, students, and teachers.

I am interested in the Curriculum Cymreig because I see it as a less useful approach to framing CE, and indeed discussions of cultural and national identity, in schools in Wales than its predecessor. The approach to discussing culture and community in *Community and Understanding* incorporated more comprehensive themes of citizenship and associated living, providing greater opportunities about the nature and role of culture and cultural identity than the current Curriculum Cymreig policy. Other scholars have felt similarly. For example, Phillips describes *Developing the Curriculum Cymreig* as "an unashamed attempt to promote the distinctive culture and heritage of Wales" (Phillips 1996,

p. 43). In 2010, I conducted a critical discourse analysis of *Developing the Curriculum Cymreig*, and my findings resonate with Phillips' perspective, and this analysis of the guidance for the Curriculum Cymreig serves as the backdrop for the studies and discussions included in Chap. 4 of this book.

Once the theoretical framework of citizenship and cultural identity was established and communicated to educators through *Community and Understanding* and its successor *Developing the Curriculum Cymreig*, the actual implementation of CE curricula in schools had to be organised and initiated. This was accomplished through two curricular endeavours situating concerns for citizenship and cultural identity in global and local perspectives: ESDGC and PSE. The promotion of ESDGC was a key objective of the Welsh Government and is still regarded as a curricular programme that prepares young people for "life in the 21st century" (ESTYN 2013 Please check ESTYN (2103) has been changed to ESTYN (2013) as per the reference list., p. 4). ESDGC is not a discrete subject for learning, but rather a philosophy or element of a school's ethos. It is a set of "values and attitudes, understanding and skills… embedded throughout school, an attitude to be adopted, a value system and way of life" (Ibid.).

The presence and health of ESDGC is evaluated and assessed by ESTYN, the inspecting body for schools in Wales. According to ESTYN, it provides advice on the quality and standards of education and training in Wales to the National Assembly and other stakeholders, and makes public findings of good practice based on inspection evidence. Inspections of ESDGC involve a school providing inspectors with a self-evaluation report generated by the head teacher and staff. The inspectors then sample evidence from the report as a means to test the claims of the school and its implementation of ESDGC practices in meeting the aims and goals of their ESDGC strategy. The supplementary guidance for ESDGC provided by ESTYN lists four general areas serving as criteria that are representative of the ways in which inspectors attempt to evaluate the presence and effectiveness of a school's ESDGC ethos. The four criteria are listed below:

1. The understanding, skills, and values held and applied by pupils of sustainable development and global citizenship
   Questions supporting this criterion relate to pupils' understanding of their actions on a local, national, and global scale. ESTYN inspectors are concerned with whether or not pupils understand people possess different approaches to, and opinions of, ESDGC and that with this understanding, pupils have the opportunity to

learn about a variety of issues in the local and wider world, including environmental, social, political, and economic issues.

2. Teaching and learning in relation to ESDGC

Concerns for teaching and learning in regard to ESDGC begin with an inspection of the PSE curriculum and its relationship to the school's ESDGC ethos. ESTYN inspectors try to identify specific connections to ESDGC in Geography and Science lessons, as well as cross-curricular applications of ESDGC across the school, similar to how schools are intended to implement the Curriculum Cymreig. Finally, ESTYN inspectors try to identify opportunities for learning ESDGC elements across Key Stages, including considerations of ESDGC in the Welsh Baccalaureate curriculum.

3. Policies and practice that promote and implement ESDGC

In addition to curricular and pedagogical elements, ESTYN inspectors are also concerned with the school's ESDGC policy—the framework that identifies strategies for how it is to develop and promote ESDGC as a prominent part of its school's ethos. This policy also includes methods of monitoring and evaluating ESDGC practices. In most cases, schools will have working groups of staff dedicated to the development of the school's implementation of ESDGC, and ESTYN is concerned with understanding how this group manages approaches to ESDGC and what the impact of the working group has in regard to improving ESDGC instruction and implementation at the school. In addition to enacting, evaluating, and developing of ESDGC policy, ESTYN inspectors look at how non-instructional factors contribute to ESDGC at the school. Extracurricular activities, healthy eating plans, and the overall effectiveness of the senior management team in understanding ESDGC are taken into consideration. This also includes questions as to whether professional development activities with direct links to ESDGC have been provided for teaching staff and what the impact of such activities has been on promoting ESDGC throughout the school.

4. Supporting the development and sustainability of ESDGC in the school

In evaluating the support and sustainability of ESDGC in a school, ESTYN inspectors are concerned with how well the staff understands ESDGC as a concept and the issues that intersect it. Along with professional development opportunities focusing on

ESDGC, inspectors are interested in ESDGC agenda items in meetings for the school governors, and feedback from teachers and other
staff to the senior management team regarding the current implementation of ESDGC and its future development.

PSE is markedly different from the ESDGC programme. PSE became
a statutory requirement for schools in September 2003 and is compulsory for all students at Key Stages 1–5. The PSE learning outcomes are
set for each Key Stage and are organised through themes of community, emotional health, environment, learning, moral concerns, physical
health, sexual health, social well-being, spiritual health, and vocation. The
Welsh Government has provided a compulsory guidance document called
the PSE Framework, which was developed in recognition of the United
Nations Convention on the Rights of the Child and the Welsh Assembly
Government's document Rights to Action, and the Education Act of
2002. Each of these policies and declarations promote the safeguard-
ing and welfare of children and young people to varying degrees, and
the PSE Framework is proposed to create an avenue for these concerns
and more through creating learning opportunities for pupils where they
can engage in conversations of personal and cultural identity set against
the backdrop of national and communal citizenship. In other words, the
PSE Framework intends to help educators "plan across the curriculum to
develop the knowledge and understanding, skills values and attitudes that
will enable learners to participate in our multi-ethnic society in Wales"
(PSE Framework 2008). Specifically, the aims of the PSE Framework are
to prepare learners to be "personally and socially effective." This is purportedly accomplished through "providing learning experiences in which
they (pupils) can develop and apply skills, explore personal attitudes and
values, and acquire appropriate knowledge and understanding" (PSE
Framework 2008). The PSE Framework lists specific curricular aims that
are intended to enable pupils to achieve "personal and social effectiveness." These aims are to…

- develop learners' self-esteem and a sense of personal responsibility
- promote self-respect, respect for others, and celebrate diversity
- equip learners to live safe, healthy lives
- prepare learners for the choices and opportunities of lifelong learning
- empower learners to participate in their schools and communities as
  active responsible citizens locally, nationally, and globally

- foster positive attitudes and behaviour towards the principles of sustainable development and global citizenship
- prepare learners for the challenges, choices, and responsibilities of work and adult life.

The PSE framework suggests its guidance provides a broad, balanced, and holistic approach to PSE, but the success of this approach is dependent upon the support given to the implementation of the PSE curriculum by the staff, the ethos of the school, and how the school is organised. In other words, the PSE Framework assumes schools will incorporate PSE outcomes as part of the overall ethos of a school, much like the ESDGC and Curriculum Cymreig policies.

In theory, approaches to citizenship through ESDGC and the PSE framework are primarily concerned with (a) active citizenship, which includes valuing diversity, understanding political processes, and participating in community and school life, and (b) sustainable development and global citizenship, which includes understanding natural resources, poverty, inequality, and global interdependence. These are important areas of learning, and, if done in ways that are sensitive to the pupils and their circumstances, can enable them to gain insightful and nuanced understandings of citizenship and democratic living. However, even with these programmes in place, discussions of culture and cultural identity framed by ESDGC and PSE curricula have the potential to be lost within a Eurocentric positioning of citizenship and community, or equally as troubling, due to the general nature in which these curricula are exercised (most notably PSE curricula as noted later on in this book), issues of culture—how it is produced, its purpose, and why we should study it have the potential to be left unconsidered in classrooms in Wales. One exception to this situation is the implementation of the Curriculum Cymreig and its potential impact on how Welshness is defined, represented, and understood by pupils.

As mentioned above, much of the research in this book is primarily interested in aspects of the Curriculum Cymreig, its composition, implementation, and potential impact on pupils' orientation to Wales, and Welshness. As the successor to *Community and Understanding*, its primary aims are to ensure young people have learning opportunities that reflect the distinctiveness of living and learning in Wales. I go into greater detail on the Curriculum Cymreig in Chaps. 3 and 4. Apart from understanding the rhetoric and implementation of the Curriculum Cymreig, it is also important to understand how the educational history of Wales has contributed to the development of this distinctively Welsh curricular policy. While the ESDGC and PSE curricular are implemented in different ways in Wales to those of the other home nations, the Curriculum Cymreig is altogether an entirely different approach to teaching citizenship and cultural identity. The current Curriculum Cymreig policy has far-reaching roots into the history of education in Wales. In the next chapter, I summarise this history and highlight the work of individuals who fought to establish the cultural, social, and political nature of cultural identity as a necessary element for schooling in Wales.

References

CCW. (1991). *Community and understanding.* Cardiff: Curriculum Council for Wales.

Daugherty, R., & Jones, S. (1999). Community, culture and identity: Geography, the National Curriculum and Wales. *The Curriculum Journal, 10*(3), 443–461.

ESTYN. (2013). *Supplementary guidance: Education for sustainable development and global citizenship.* Cardiff: ESTYN.

Frazer, E. (1999). Introduction: The idea of political education: Towards curriculum reform. *Oxford Review of Education, 25*(1–2), 5–22.

Jowell, R., & Park, A. (1998). *Young people, politics and citizenship: A disengaged generation?* London: The Citizenship Foundation.

Kymlicka, W. (1996). *Multicultural citizenship: A liberal theory of minority rights.* Oxford: Oxford University Press.

Mair, P. (2008). The challenge to party government. *West European Politics, 3*(1&2), 211–234.

Marsh, D., O'Toole, T., & Jones, S. (2007). *Young people and politics in the UK: Apathy or alienation?* Basingstoke: Palgrave.

Pattie, C., Seyd, P., & Whiteley, P. (2004). *Citizenship in Britain: Values, participation and democracy.* Cambridge: Cambridge University Press.

Phillips, R. (1996). History teaching, cultural restorationism and national identity in England and Wales. *Curriculum Studies, 4*(3), 385–399.

Phillps, R., & Daugherty, R. (2000). Educational devolution and nation building in Wales: A different 'Great Debate?' in Furlong, J., & Phillips, R. (2001). *Education, reform and the state: Twenty five years of politics, policy and practice.* London: Routledge. pp. 87–100.

Sloam, J. (2007). Rebooting democracy: Youth participation in politics the UK. *Parliamentary Affairs, 60*(4), 548–567.

Stoker, G., & Hay, C. (2009). Revitalising politics: Have we lost the plot? *Representation, 45*(3), 225–236.

Watson, J. (2004). Educating for citizenship: The emerging relationship between religious education and citizenship education. *British Journal of Religious Education, 26*(3), 259–271.

Welsh Government. (2008). PSE Framework. Retrieved August, 2015 from http://learning.gov.wales/docs/learningwales/publications/130425-personal-and-social-education-framework-en.pdf

Young, I. (2002). *Inclusion and democracy*. Oxford: Oxford University Press.

CHAPTER 2

A Brief History of Education in Wales

Abstract Smith provides a brief history of education in Wales, emphasising how the hegemonic relationship with England continues to contribute to contemporary curricular development. Additionally, Smith highlights how cultural restorationism has existed as an organisational theme in the continued development of an educational system in Wales. A discussion of key figures who sought to establish sustainable schooling in Wales, while still being subjected to larger concerns of church, state, personal ambition, and, at times, Welsh culture and language, highlights the intersectionality of curriculum, culture, and politics. Ultimately, this history provides the context for the establishment of the national curriculum for Wales in the 1980s, the development of the Curriculum Cymreig, and eventual devolution of educational powers to Wales in the 1990s.

Keywords Cultural restorationism • Curriculum Cymreig • Welsh education • Welsh language • Devolution

Much of the interest in CE in Wales stems from devolutionary powers granted to Wales in the late 1990s. However, concerns over the interplay between schooling and national and cultural identity have been central to educational concerns in Wales for centuries. In this chapter, I give a brief summary of the educational history of Wales and highlight a handful of individuals who not only strove for a quality system of education in Wales, but were also driven by concerns to maintain Wales and Welshness in school.

© The Editor(s) (if applicable) and The Author(s) 2016   11
K. Smith, *Curriculum, Culture and Citizenship Education in Wales*,
DOI 10.1057/978-1-137-54443-8_2

The history of Wales is more than an account of a single country or nation; it is the history of a multiplicity of people, power, and perspectives that have all contributed to contemporary Wales. From its first recognition as a country with a people, Wales has been subjected to one form of domination or another. For example, the contemporary indigenous term for Wales, the name of the country in its native tongue, is Cymru. This is derived from the Brythonic term *Cambrogi*, which means "fellow countrymen" (Davies 1990). The term "Wales," however, is a derivative of the Saxon word *Waelas* and was taken up by the Welsh, Latin-speaking clergy in the twelfth century and translates to "foreigner" (Jenkins 2007). By the early twelfth century, those who wrote about and for Wales were referring to their "fellow countrymen" as "foreigners." Is this the beginning of the influence of English imperialism in Wales? It is impossible to know for sure, but it does serve as an indicator of the antiquity of the struggle Wales has experienced in determining its cultural presence and place as a nation and people. If the adoption of a foreign name as a moniker of a nation is an indication of the future of colonisation in Wales, then perhaps the development of devolutionary powers in Wales is an indication of a new future. On 31 July 1998, the Government of Wales Act was passed, which in turn brought into existence a devolved legislative body of government called the National Assembly for Wales. Apart from the significance of the political and cultural ramifications of this event, and in considering the long and sometimes difficult history that has developed between England and Wales, the institution of the National Assembly had a profound effect on education in Wales. It was from this point forward that Wales would eventually develop its own educational philosophy in determining the goals and methods that the government would employ in meeting the needs of its citizenry. Most important, for the first time since the Acts of Union in 1536–1542, these goals and aims would bear a meaningful and distinct differentiation from those of England as policymakers and politicians claimed a devolved government would seek to meet the social, cultural, and economic needs of people in Wales.

The process of devolution in Wales continues still, with arguments for and against the ultimate state of possible independence from England. With these arguments come larger ramifications in terms of economy, culture, and, in particular, education policy. There are a number of excellent sources detailing the emergence of a devolved Welsh educational system and its continued development. The devolution of educational governance to Wales is one of, if not the most, significant episodes of the history of education in Wales. However, irrespective of its significance, my focus is not on the detailed implications of educational devolution. Instead, I hope to demonstrate how some individuals over the centuries have worked to introduce quality education in Wales and while maintaining a Welsh identity through schooling in the face of cultural hegemony and domination. The history of education in Wales is a story of struggle framed in a web of religious, political, cultural, and economic pressures. Historically, certain challenges existed in the form of inadequate materials, deplorable facilities, and poorly trained teachers, who although had a desire to teach, simply were not provided with adequate instruction commensurate to their needs or the needs of their pupils. In addition, ideological struggles and misconceived notions of who deserves an education, and for what reasons, further complicated the development of a viable, well-constructed system of education. The remnants of this historical reality still, to a degree, mitigate the educational success of pupils in Wales. Over the years, educational leaders in Wales have acknowledged this fact, and as Wales has struggled to develop a globally recognised national identity, on its own terms, in the European Union (and even in the UK), these leaders have attempted to make a positive impact on the efficacy of education in Wales at large, as well as contribute to the richness of the individual experience of the pupil.

What follows is a brief, and admittedly, incomplete description of the history of education in Wales. In this summary, I address key historical periods and specifically discuss individuals that contributed to the development of a system of public education in Wales and the eventual creation of the Curriculum Cymreig. These individuals valued the distinctiveness of Welsh culture and possessed the desire to develop an educational presence that would ultimately open the doors to devolution and the localised governance of education in Wales. I emphasise the contributions of these individuals, as opposed to writing a broad narrative of educational history in Wales because their stories assist in illustrating the actions made by real individuals in the political struggles of two nations vying for the control of a method of constructing, reproducing, and communicating the culture of a people—struggles which are often rendered so abstract that the efforts of the individuals could be lost in a "historical haze." Additionally, I would be remiss if I did not mention the absence of women in this summation of the history of Welsh education. Unfortunately, little is said of the women who laboured to ensure quality education for pupils in Wales. In cases where they are mentioned, they are often simply attached to charismatic male figures who are vaunted as champions of their cause. However, in reality, I am sure there are as many women (or more) with as many (or more) compelling stories as the men described in the paragraphs that follow. Finally, I draw attention to the fact that the desire to include Welsh culture as a distinctive element in the education of the Welsh people was in direct response to elements of English imperialism transmitted through centuries of colonisation of Wales by England, with one of the instruments of empire being made manifest in the forms of Anglican philanthropy and carried out through multiple iterations of English educational policy.

EARLY HISTORY AND THE MEDIEVAL AGES

This description of the early history of education in Wales begins in the fifth century. At this point in time, the Romans had successfully subdued the Welsh populace for over 300 years and, although the Romans would soon withdraw from Britain, a precedent for the linguistic impact of the Romans had been established. While Latin was established as the language of religion and law, Cymraeg (their native tongue) was used by the majority of the Welsh in their everyday lives (Jenkins 2007). At the end of the fifth century, the Romans left Wales, but their influence remained with the introduction of Christianity and the use of Latin as the ecclesiastical language of the church (Jones and Roderick 2003). In terms of education, life in Wales during the fifth century largely consisted of subsistence farming and agriculturally based trade (Jenkins 2007). In this environment, education for the common folk (Gwerin or "y 'Werin" in Cymraeg) did not occur in classrooms. Rather, it occurred between fathers and sons in the fields, mothers and daughters in the home, and other non-familial, social relationships in the villages and towns that dotted the Welsh landscape. Formal education began with the monks of the early Celtic Church. Illtud, a fifth-century monk, founded an institution for learning in south Wales drawing disciples from as far as Brittany (Williams and Hughes 1978). However, this form of education was not extended to "y 'Werin," as literacy was the purview of clerics. From this perspective, literacy was necessary for the propagation of the gospel, but not for the saving of souls. For hundreds of years the monks would continue studying and copying their sacred texts, while Welsh kings and princes would rule over their respective kingdoms. During these years, an emphasis on oral histories and traditions gave rise to the role of the bard, an individual who underwent long and thorough training in poetry and genealogy (Jenkins 2007), and the lawyer, who also trained orally and assisted kings and lords in interpreting the law. Bards were afforded places of honour and responsibility in the courts of the king and his lords, as they were the guardians of the whole corpus of the traditional lore of the royal family and the people they ruled (Williams and Hughes 1978). Lawyers were also well respected, but did not receive the acclaim that accompanied the bard. Another example of the value of oral traditions is found in the guilds where skilled instruction was shared with apprentices and guild members and carefully guarded from those outside of the guild. This guardianship of knowledge ensured a demand for services rendered and also protected lines of economic and social mobility from the general populace. The emphasis on the bardic tradition, study of the law and religion, and the role of the guilds are made known in the Law of Hywel the Good (Cyfraith am Hywel Dda, c. 880–950).

> There are three arts which a villain may not teach his son without the lord's permission, scholarship, bardism and smithcraft; because if his lord permits the scholar to wear a tonsure, or a smith to enter a smithy, or a bard to sing, then no one can afterwards enslave them. (Jenkins 1986, p. 19)

In this short passage, the importance of education as a vehicle for social mobility and liberation, as well as a method of excising oneself from the complete influence of the king or lord, is made manifest. However, as the administration of royal affairs grew more complex and early medieval life of people in Wales met challenging circumstances, the emphasis for oral traditions was lessened and the desire for a formalised, text based form of education increased.

REBELLION, REFORMATION, AND RENAISSANCE

As time passed from the Dark Ages into the latter part of the Medieval Ages, three calamities would come to affect the development of formal education in Wales (Jones and Roderick 2003). The first of these instances came with the conquest of Wales by Edward I in 1282. With the coming of an English King came the death of Llewelyn ap Grufydd, the last native prince of Wales, and any notion of Welsh self-government. The conquest of Edward I started the eventual colonisation of Wales and anglicisation of Welsh culture. The second calamity was the "Black Death," which killed approximately one-third of the population in Wales (Jenkins 2007). The Black Death was no respecter of persons. The clergy who travelled throughout Wales serving the laity of the hamlets and villages throughout the country also suffered from its effects. As a result, the ranks of literate clergy were devastated, and those who did remain most often copied existing holy scripture without developing new intellectual contributions (Jones and Roderick 2003). Moreover, fears of infection ran unchecked, and as a result religious institutions were less likely to accept new scholars. Consequently, the body of scholars in Wales shrank in numbers. The final significant development of the Middle Ages affecting formal education was the defeat of the Welsh rebellion led by Owain Glyndwr in the fifteenth century. The circumstances of the life of Owain Glyndwr are shrouded in mystery. There is no record of his birth or where he died (Jenkins 2007). Shakespeare described him as "not in the roll of common men" and in Henry IV he had King Henry refer to Glyndwr as "that great magician, damn'd Glendower" (Shakespeare 2005). The reality of Glyndwr would prove equally intriguing. He was the son of an affluent nobleman, had served in the English army, and even spilled Celtic blood (Jenkins 2007, p. 111). He "became the most impressive and eloquent defender of the right of the Welsh people" (Ibid.) and was proclaimed Prince of Wales by a group of devoted followers in Glyndyfrdwy, Edeirnon, in Merioneth (Jenkins 2007). As Glyndwr grew in power and influence, his desire for Welsh independence also increased. Convinced with the righteousness of his cause, he waged guerrilla warfare against the English state in the mid-1400s. The Welsh uprising disrupted many facets of life in Wales. English forces gathered a larger presence, resources were diverted to support the war, and tensions between the English state and Wales worsened and never truly recovered. Apart from the disruptions of war, the economic recovery that followed the Black Death and Glyndwr uprising placed a focus on crafts and literature which not only prompted a change in methods of training for bards, but also opened the doors to a broader distribution of skilled instruction for labourers (Jones and Roderick 2003). In addition to these economic developments came a greater need for lawyers who could help arbitrate the law during these prosperous times. However, the training of lawyers had to change in order to meet the growing demand for written records. In previous years kings and lords depended on bards and lawyers, who were orally trained in poetry, genealogy, and law, for the administration of their kingdoms. However, in the latter part of the Medieval Ages, the complications of administering "the king's justice" required literacy as well as knowledge of the traditions of the land and royal house (Jones and Roderick 2003). Situated between the horror of the "Black Death" and the violence of Glyndwr's revolution, a lawyer by the name of David Holbache and his wife Guinevere founded a grammar school in Oswestry, Wales, in 1407. The Holbaches had no official affiliation with any religious denomination and are described as possessing a "vision and love of learning which characterized this early period of the Renaissance" (Jenkins 2007). Instances such as this challenged the churches' dominion over education at the time and also contributed to the growing disparity between land owners, those who could afford to attend schools, and their tenant, landless labourers.

The role of the church in education would change rapidly in the sixteenth and seventeenth century, particularly as it would undergo a massive transformation via the apparatus of the state (and, in particular, the influence of Henry VIII). Latin had remained as the language of the church, and, as such, Welsh parishioners would essentially attend services fully conducted in a foreign tongue. At this point participation in religious rites relied entirely on recognition of a few choice words and graphic representations of the gospel. However, as the Reformation swept through Britain, the visual elements of the services—stained glass windows, iconography of the Virgin Mary, and depictions of pilgrimages were almost entirely removed (Jones and Roderick 2003). The priests and worshippers were now left with little more than catechisms and litanies that were of little use to those who did not have a strong grasp of Latin. It was becoming increasingly apparent to Welsh worshippers and clergy alike that reading the scriptures in their own tongue was the only way to real salvation.

The English state also understood the power of literacy and the potential it possessed in providing pathways to greater freedom and liberation. During his reign in the early sixteenth century, Henry VIII decreed that "the bible should only be read by the aristocracy, gentry, and prosperous merchants" (Ibid). In addition, Henry VIII enacted the Chantries Act of 1547 which placed all chantries under control of the king. While this was problematic for the local clergy, it was even more devastating to the poor people of their parishes who would no longer have access to what little education they received through the church. Apart from these complications, the scriptures existed as the most common reading material of the time, and Welsh clergy continued to believe that the inability to read the scriptures would not only threaten the eternal salvation of the Welsh, but also keep them ignorant and out of touch with the economic and political developments of the day. Thus, in 1588 Bishop William Morgan arranged for the translation of the Bible into Welsh, a relatively simple undertaking which would transform the religious and educational landscape of Wales. As the sixteenth century progressed, the position of the state and upper class regarding the poor lower class members was greatly influenced by the development of, and appreciation for, culture inspired by the Renaissance.

However, in regard to the lower class, education continued to be a primary function of the church. In opposition to her father's views, Queen Elizabeth viewed reading the Bible as a necessary tool in the battle for people's souls. In addition, many upper class citizens developed charitable organisations which served to establish grammar schools through England and Wales for the poorer citizenry. These philanthropic efforts were the result of the double-edged sword of Puritanism which led to the acquisition of greater wealth on one hand and the need for charitable service on the other. Through these philanthropic efforts, a handful of privately funded grammar schools continued to operate in Wales from the sixteenth century into the seventeenth century. The curriculum of these schools reflected that of the ancient universities and church schools in England and focused on classical instruction, with all instruction held in English. The focus of studies was on the Latin and Greek languages, and relied on memorisation and learning by rote rather than the dialectical method of instruction found in the Medieval Ages (Jones and Roderick 2003).

In 1650 the Act for the Better Preaching and Propagation of the Gospel in Wales contributed to a larger perspective on the education and spiritual needs of the Welsh. This Puritan-led programme established 60 grammar schools throughout Wales. Although short-lived, this educational initiative incorporated the international view of Comenius, a Swedish theologian and educator who "believed that education should be provided from infancy, first in the home, then in the village school, then in the city gymnasium, and finally at university" (Jones 2003, p. 18). Comenius also shared the Lutheran notion that education should not be grounded in narrow classicism, but instead should serve as a preparation for life. A Puritan educational philosophy also included the influences of Hartlib and Dury who viewed education as a means for saving souls and a safeguard against the sins of idleness and profanity (Jones and Roderick 2003). Although well intentioned, these endeavours were constructed on ideas born from the urban areas of England and translated poorly into the rural reality of the Welsh.

For most Welsh, both the language and experience of formal education were a foreign concept that alienated them to a degree from the concepts they were intending to learn. If the formal education of the Welsh was to succeed, it seemed that there must be a movement born within Wales that radiated outwards from the lived circumstances of the people and not a prescribed method of English assimilation. Undoubtedly, the most important educational development to arise from the seventeenth century was the organisation of the Welsh Trust by Thomas Gouge, an English Puritan minister who was ejected from the clergy in London. In 1674, he established a charitable organisation that provided a network of over 300 schools throughout Wales (National Library of Wales 2009). Although his death in 1681 marked the end of the Welsh Trust movement, it inspired the creation of another charitable organisation that would have an even more significant contribution to early education in Wales.

In 1699 the Society for the Promotion of Christian Knowledge (SPCK) was created. This organisation quickly established a nationwide network of Anglican charity schools across Wales. For the next 40 years, the SPCK would continue to develop schools expanding upon the regularly used "grammar school" curriculum. It was during this period of time that the first noted "Welsh hero" of education emerged. This figure would not only lead to the broadening of the Welsh philosophy of education, but he would also contribute to the shifting of Welsh religion from the main body of the Anglican Church (the Nonconformist movement), a shift that had far-reaching cultural and political significance in Wales.

THE ACTS OF UNION AND CYMRAEG IN SCHOOLS

The establishment of the Anglican Church as the church of the state had a large impact in terms of developing a system of education in Wales. Charitable and church-led organisations, including Catholic, Presbyterian, and Anglican groups, would each vie for the salvation of Welsh souls and the monetary donations of the people who possessed them. In addition to these movements, other important developments in the form of national legislation developed during the reign of Henry Tudor (VII). These initiatives would then be further expanded and established by his descendant Henry VIII. These actions would also have long-lasting effects on Welsh education and society at large. With the ascendancy of Henry VIII to the throne of England came sweeping changes to the political relationship between Wales and England. The changes produced effects that persevered through the ages and were firmly situated at the very heart of curriculum development in Wales in the twentieth century.

From 1536, the Acts of Union would have a profound effect on the lives of the Welsh. Through the Acts, the English crown assumed full control of Wales. This granted a benefit to the Welsh people in that they could now be represented in parliament. However, the cons far outweighed the pros, with perhaps the greatest detriment taking the form of English becoming the official language of the realm. Welsh could no longer be used in state-controlled venues, meaning Welsh could not be spoken in parliament, court proceedings, marriages, or any other official state discourse (such as buying or selling land or paying taxes). At the time, Wales was predominately a monoglot country with the vast majority of its citizenry capable of speaking only Cymraeg. This legislation effectively rendered them quite literally subjects to the crown, with no recognised access or appeal to the law in their native language. Although these events occurred in the sixteenth century, I will briefly describe how this attitude towards Cymraeg matured in schools, with the effects continuing to shape a more contemporary educational policy.

The institutionalisation of prejudice against the Welsh language gave legitimacy to the belief that the Welsh were simple, parochial, and unrefined (Jenkins 2007). As English was the language of modernity, Cymraeg was the tongue of the native, and it had no place in the future of Britain. As the years rolled on, this perspective regarding Cymraeg bled into nearly every aspect of Welsh life. English became the language of the workplace, the schoolyard, and eventually the home. This phenomenon is a practical example of one aspect of hegemony (Gramcsi 1971)—no swords, bayonets, or guns were used in the near elimination of Cymraeg. Instead, many Welsh speakers were compelled by the rhetoric of the English government and the discursive practices, which both produced and reproduced the dominancy of the English language, and voluntarily abandoned Welsh. The consensual attack on the Welsh language took many forms and lasted for centuries. For example, in primary schools during the eighteenth and nineteenth century, teachers, administrators, and pupils alike participated in a practice that came to be called the "Welsh Not." If a child spoke Welsh in the classroom, he or she would receive the "Welsh Not"—a small wooden placard on a lanyard worn around the neck. If the child continued to speak Welsh, he or she would be whipped by the schoolmaster. In addition, if pupils heard their schoolmates speaking Welsh in the yard, they were encouraged to tell the teacher or headmaster and would be rewarded with sweets and the like for their actions. In my own family history, stories of my great-grandfather wearing the *Cwstom*, or *Welsh Not*, were handed down as a novelty of their schooling experience. Oddly, as these stories were told, there was little consideration as to the effects of this process, even though there are no members of my family who speak Welsh as a familial or community language. In fact, even with Welsh as a second language as a compulsory element in schools in Wales, none of my family—including cousins, nephews, and nieces—consider themselves fluent or actively communicate in Welsh.

According to Jenkins (2007), at the time of the 1901 census roughly 80% of the Welsh population in mid and west Wales (what Balsom referred to as *Y fro Gymraeg* in his "three Wales Model") spoke Cymraeg. However, by 1951 the percentage of Welsh speakers in Wales was reduced to less than 29%. Throughout the history of Welsh education, many educators and those concerned with Welsh education and culture observed this decline with dismay. Many of the changes that have occurred in recent years in Welsh education have been primarily concerned with the reclamation of Cymraeg. The Welsh language was recognised as an official language in the UK in 1993 (Welsh Language Act 1993), and in 2001, the number of people speaking Cymraeg in Wales increased for the first time since the census of 1901 (Jenkins 2007). Since the Welsh Language Act of 1993, Welsh has become a compulsory subject in schools in Wales, and many schools are bilingual or wholly Welsh medium environments. Whereas in previous years educators and clergy were concerned with the salvation of the souls of the Welsh, many influential contemporary educational authorities regarded Cymraeg as the spirit of Welshness and were concerned with saving the soul of Wales itself.

Philanthropy and Nonconformity

Griffith Jones (1684–1761), who served as the rector of Llanddowror, was driven by strong convictions to preach the gospel. However, he could not ignore what he called the "extremely miserable blindness" of his own country. Initially, he attempted to overcome this blindness through preaching, but he would soon write "how deplorably ignorant the poor people are who cannot read, even where constant preaching is not wanting, while catechising is omitted" (Gittins 1954, p. 13). Jones had a talent for preaching, but perhaps an even greater talent in procuring funding for his vision of a school that enabled Christians to not only read, but also understand the scriptures and, in particular, the catechisms of the church. Sir John Phillips of Picton Castle, an original member of the SPCK, was Jones' initial grant source. However, Phillips' death in 1737 would eventually lead to Jones developing a relationship with Madam Bridget Bevan, who proved to be a close friend and staunch supporter who worked with Jones through the remainder of his life. The success of the Circulating Schools of the SPCK movement was built upon the shrewdness of Jones in financial matters, as well as his ability to transform the curriculum to better meet the needs of Welsh pupils. The teaching was in both English and Welsh, and the SPCK also published and distributed a Welsh Bible. While this was not illegal, it was not something that the Church of England supported. This work was achieved primarily through the efforts of a Welsh Bishop name William Morgan (1541–1604), who is credited with contributing to the survival of the Welsh language (Jenkins 2007; Jones and Roderick 2003) through the publication of a Welsh translation of the Bible. In addition to basic literacy and the catechism, boys were taught arithmetic. Girls who attended the school would learn needlework, spinning, and weaving. Although the schools were set up in a wide variety of buildings, annual inspections kept the standards to a relatively high level. By 1761, the year of Jones' death, it is estimated that 150,000 were taught in approximately 3300 schools throughout Wales (Gittins 1954). This number does not represent the adult pupils who eventually attended the schools, a practice unheard of in earlier years.

The educational, religious, and even political influences of Jones would be felt for years after his death. For example, Thomas Charles (1755–1814), a fellow Welshman from Carmarthenshire, regarded Jones as his mentor, even though Charles was only six years old when Jones died in 1761. In considering the impact and goal of Charles' mission for creating a system of schooling in Wales, Gittins references a quote from the eighteenth century regarding the future of Wales, "'Pwy a gyfyd Gymru, canys bechau yw?' By whom shall Wales be raised, for she is small?" (Gittins 1954, p. 31). Who is the caretaker of the Welsh pupils' scholarship and salvation, and what are the ramifications if this stewardship is lost? This question is important in that people in Wales could now take the biblical accounts of what they were reading and apply it to their own lives (the quote referenced above was a question the prophet Amos had asked regarding the Israelites), and also that they possessed a shared faith in the moral uplift of Wales that would come about by the hand of God manifested through the education of the Welsh, and it is in these circumstances that Thomas Charles entered the field of education. Charles attended the dissenting Academy in Carmarthen, an institution descended from a Nonconformist tradition. Throughout his training, Charles associated with Calvinists and Unitarians, and ultimately with Methodists while at the Academy. It was during his associations with the Methodists that he considered himself to be saved (Gittins 1954).

However, even with his eternal salvation in hand, the reality of Charles' mortal life was marked by periods of trouble—particularly financial trouble. His studies at Oxford following the Academy in Carmarthen were marked by financial embarrassments. Moreover, once returning to Wales he had difficulty in establishing a living in Bala, a city in the rural northern portion of Wales. He did, however, marry well, and it was this union that brought him not only financial peace, but also an opportunity to develop social connections with other Methodists in the area. His marriage to Miss Sally Jones of Bala marks the second appearance of a well-financed woman who contributed to the success of education in Wales, but whose mention is only accompanied by that of her "heroic" husband. When Charles joined the Methodist movement in Bala, it was a movement in crisis. Charles was motivated to preserve this tradition since this was the pathway to his own salvation.

However, he recognised, as did Jones before him, that preaching to an illiterate populace could not result in the saving of souls. With the circulating schools established by Jones going bankrupt with the death of Madam Bevan in 1778, Welsh pupils had little opportunity to attend free schools (or schools with a limited fee structure). Therefore, Charles felt his first task was to educate the people, and so he established his own charity schools to accomplish this task. Charles followed Jones' example through hiring untrained teachers, training them himself, and then paying them on a modest scale. However, his greatest success (educationally speaking) was in expanding the curriculum established by Jones.

Where Jones rigidly believed in the catechism as the primary source of salvation, and therefore the core component of his educational philosophy, Charles incorporated more of a pragmatic approach. The popularity of his schools was predicated on the fact that there was no fixed curriculum applied to all schools. There were particular features which were found in all schools, but in areas that demonstrated particular needs, Charles adopted "extended facilities" and experimented with various methods of instruction and content areas that would work to meet those demands (Gittins 1954). In addition, Charles' schools were socially inclusive. This is not to say that children with mental, emotional, or physical disabilities were attending the school, or that differentiated instruction took place, but rather that the schools were not confined to serving the children of the labouring classes. Thus, it was possible that children of the local gentry sat next to those who were working in their fathers' fields directly after school let out. Additionally, Charles placed a greater emphasis on additional reading material than just the Bible. Finally, Charles had developed a coherent theory regarding the use of the Welsh language in teaching (Gittins 1954). He believed, and was able to prove through the educational outcomes of his pupils, that literacy in Welsh did not hinder literacy in English (as was commonly believed at the time), but rather literacy in one language worked in establishing literacy in a second language.

Charles held lessons on Sunday afternoons, allowing parents to send their children to school without sacrificing labour needed around the home or farm. These Sunday Schools were managed by a democracy of teachers (Gittins 1954) which contributed to a wide variety of educational methods that were elastic enough to meet the various needs of the populations they served. These factors, along with the fact that Charles operated as the architect of the Welsh Calvinistic Methodist denomination, created a demand for the Sunday Schools that surpassed the notoriety of the SPCK schools. This Nonconformist movement swelled on the educational growth of the pupils of the Sunday Schools and led to a unique form of worship that was equal parts nationalism and spiritualism. Through the Nonconformist movement, education was highlighted as a means to spiritual enlightenment and social and civic understanding and responsibility. Not only did the individual curricula strive to meet the needs of the local constituencies, but the teachers also practised democratic methods that could be observed as a model of successful social living for the pupils and community. These concepts and practices are important features of a nation looking to establish itself from a long and drawn-out crisis of cultural and political renewal. As Jones notes in his lecture referred to earlier, "Charles' motto might have been, 'Canus nid oes i ni yma ddinas barhaus, eithr un i ddyfod yr ŷm yn ei ddisgwl': For we have not here an abiding city, but we hope for one to come" (Gittins 1954, p. 54).

TREASON IN VICTORIAN TIMES

The hope for "an abiding" Wales came for many in the form of the industrial revolution of the nineteenth century. In many parts of Wales, the economic influx developed by coal and steel eventually translated into educational attainment and some semblance of financial stability and social mobility. With the development of industry came the infusion of people into the valleys of Wales. In the latter part of the century, the population of cities such as Merthyr Tydfil would more than double in size, leading to poverty, disease, and political unrest. In these times, only 70% of children aged 8 through 12 attended school, while many children (some as young as 7 years of age) were sent to work (Jones and Roderick 2003). With the majority of education still existing as a voluntary endeavour, the Nonconformists viewed the increasing funding from the English government as a method of developing greater state control and influence of the established Anglican Church over education. Nonconformity was rapidly evolving as not only a religious, but also a political movement that promoted Welsh culture and independence.

Moreover, many Nonconformists believed in the transformational power of education as the vehicle for political and cultural viability for Wales. However, none of the Nonconformists who shared this perspective would have as much influence on the education of the Welsh as Hugh Owen. Hugh Owen (1804–1881), who was a central figure in not only improving the educational provisions offered in Wales, but he also sought to address what he believed were attacks on Welsh culture from educational "experts" from England (Gittins 1954). He was born on the isle of Anglesey, far removed from the southern villages that were soon to be ravaged by the onslaught of industry. Owen was bred in the Methodist tradition and eventually influenced by Calvinist preaching. At the age of 21 he learned shorthand and left Anglesey to work in the office of a Welsh lawyer in London. He enjoyed varied success while in London and was eventually married. His wife, however, could not withstand Welsh sermons and eventually joined a Baptist church. Owen soon joined as well. All of these experiences attributed to his undogmatic religious beliefs, which, although strong, did not dominate the scope of his educational philosophy as it did that of his predecessors. He was not overly concerned with the saving of souls as much as he was concerned with the preservation of the Welsh language and culture.

While in London, Owen became Chairman of the National Temperance League and many other charitable organisations. He also became further involved in political matters in London and assisted Benjamin Disraeli in the preparation of his Reform Bill (Jenkins 2007). While Owen established himself politically, the disparity existing between the urban and rural areas of Wales was becoming more and more apparent. In developed areas of Wales successful schools were positioned in areas of economic growth and stability, while schools which were inadequate were cast against a much more dismal background of industrial pollution, outbreaks of dysentery and cholera, and unchecked poverty. Isolated schools in remote districts faced their own difficulties. "A Welsh language culture enjoyed its extramural existence, but it is the degree of isolation, mental, emotional, even fashionable isolation, which distinguished the more from the less developed regions" (Gittins 1954, p. 74). In both cases of deprivation, the general population lacked access to dignity and respectability. Owen was committed to the notion of respectability, and in turn felt it was necessary to make Wales respectable as well and to bring it into modern society. Motivated by what many Nonconformists felt was the encroachment of England and the Anglican Church upon the domain of Welsh education, Owen engaged in a political tour de force. His desire to see Wales develop into a respectable nation served as his primary motivation. Utilising his Methodist connections in Wales, and the power associated with the various roles he held in organisations, Owen sought to rally the Nonconformist forces against the onslaught of the Anglican Church. The first forays would come in the form of educational grants for schools in Wales, which roughly equated to English funds for schools that privileged an English perspective. However, the main thrust of the struggle would come in 1847 through the *Reports of the Commissioners of Inquiry into the State of Education in Wales*, or what the Welsh referred to as *Brad y Llyfrau Gleision* (the treachery of the Blue Books, a reference to the blue covers of the reports). Owen's response was manifested in editorials, academic articles, and blistering political rhetoric that decried the validity and intent of the report.

William Williams, the MP from Coventry at the time, claimed that an improved school system was necessary to establish order in what he regarded to be the chaotic, wild regions of Wales. According to Roberts, Williams argued that "education was a cheaper and easier way of creating an obedient population than the use of force" and that "the moral power of the schoolmaster was a more economical and effectual instrument in governing this people than the bayonet" (Roberts 1998, p. 24). Williams possessed the view of the Welsh being backwards, parochial, and of a different class of people altogether—a sentiment that had been nurtured through centuries of domination by the English. In explaining his rationale for the "Blue Books," Williams stated, that without the "fostering hand of Government," the Welsh will "inevitably continue as... the most degraded and benighted of Her Majesty's subjects" (Kreider 2002, p. 31). When published, the contents of the "Blue Books" contained accurate depictions of the deplorable state of education throughout the majority of

Wales, as well as truthful descriptions of the desire for many Welsh pupils to learn. For example, J.C. Symons, one of three authors of the report, wrote:

> I can speak in very strong terms of the natural ability and capacity for instructions of the Welsh people. Though they are ignorant, no people more richly deserve to be educated. In the first place, they desire it to the full extent of their power to appreciate it; in the next, their natural capacity is of a high order, especially in the Welsh districts. They learn what they are even badly taught with surprising facility. Their memories are very retentive, and they are remarkably shrewd in catching an idea. In the words of a clergyman who has lived among them, they "see what you mean before you have said it." (Lingen et al. 1847, p. 57)

However, the most important content of the "Blue Books" were the significant anti-Welsh sentiments demonstrated by each of the authors. In the reports, the moral and cultural qualities of the Welsh were under constant attack. Symons, who wrote so positively of the Welsh people's educability, would also argue that

> there are few countries where the standard of minor morals is lower... Petty thefts, lying, cozening, every species of chicanery, drunkenness... and idleness prevail... among the least educated part of the community, who scarcely regard them in the light of sins. (Lingen et al. 1847, p. 57)

The other commissioners were equally insulting, if not more so, and through their vitriol the intent of the report as an instrument of denigrating the Welsh would provide justification for the restructuring of their educational system and attempts to replace the ideals of nonconformity with Anglican dogma and Cymreig with the language of prosperity—English. Thus, although the report did reveal the inadequacies of Welsh education, it also operated as a method to perpetuate the colonisation of Wales and an effort to establish the cultural assimilation of the Welsh to an English norm (Smith 2007). In previous work, I have written about how a system of public education in Wales was developed where a nationalised curriculum decidedly based on English history and identity displaced historically and culturally aware curricula in Wales, with the possible result being the continued marginalisation and "othering" of the Welsh. Bohata underscores this concern in writing the following:

> The psychological analyses of the colonial situation by Fanon, Memmi,
> and others is useful in understanding the Welsh experience, where the
> Welsh sense of inferiority described by Thomas and Williams is instilled
> (in part) by the internalization of negative English/British perceptions
> and constructions of Welsh, as well as by a version of history which shows
> Welsh defeat as an inevitable phase in the progressive march of civilization.
> (Bohata 2004, p. 24)

Throughout the history of Welsh education, the presence of English imperialism is readily apparent as the systems of public education are infiltrated by state-endorsed curricula and policies which alienate marginalised cultures and histories and render them subordinate to the correctness of the dominant, imperialist definition of culture, citizenship, and worth. The "Blue Books" were commissioned near the zenith of the British Empire, and this imperial attitude was exercised not only against native peoples in India and Africa, but also in the small country to the west of England. However, this attitude was not met with silence. Hugh Owen orchestrated written responses, protests, and other forms of public outcry against the moral judgements of the commissioners. He also used their findings on the state of education to further his own agenda of creating a respectable and modern Wales. From a curricular perspective, Owens was no visionary, and as an educator, he was more of an organiser and facilitator than one who understood the best ways in which pupils learn. However, it was these abilities as an administrator that allowed him to make transformational change in the educational landscape of Wales.

With support largely coming from the Nonconformist middle class, Owen established an educational scheme that was to be, in his words, "a harmonious whole" (Gittins 1954, p. 80). The system contained primary schools as a base, and then secondary schools. Old schools were refurbished and new schools were built. The system was largely funded by the fees generated from the schools. In addition, Owen devised local scholarships that were intended to "catch the exceptionally bright children of the poor" (Gittins 1954, p. 81). These scholarships were awarded to primary school children and would give a place at secondary school for two years. In addition to the existing curricula already in place in schools, the aspiration of a modern Wales also incorporated the inclusion of vocational training, resulting in mining schools, and training for working in the ironworks. In the figure of Owen we see a range of contradictions and paradoxes; he was Welsh born, but empowered through English law, a multitude of religious influences, and a general lack of understanding in educational methods, but a skilled administrator of educational processes and resources. With these characteristics, Owen provided a firm foundation from which future workers in Welsh education could operate.

Owen Edwards was one such worker. Born in 1858 in Wales, Edwards would rise to hold the office of the Chief Inspector of Education for Wales. In this office, he would have a lasting impact on the structure of the educational system in Wales and a meaningful and long-lasting contribution to the importance of Welsh culture as a component a nation's curriculum. Edwards' cultural sensitivity may have been influenced by his attending Ysgol y Llan, a "Welsh Not" school which punished pupils for speaking Cymraeg. Eventually he would attend Coleg y Bala (a theological college in the hometown of Thomas Charles) as a lay student. While in Coleg y Bala, he earned an entrance scholarship to Aberystwyth College. Edwards preached during his time in Aberystwyth but was not confident of his abilities. Eventually, he would attend Glasgow University briefly, and from there he would eventually lecture at Oxford, and it was during these years that his work for Wales would begin.

In 1889 Edwards would begin work as an editor for five periodicals: *Cymru* (*Wales*), *Cymru'r Plant* (*The Welsh Child*), *Wales*, *Heddiw* (*Today*), and *Y Llenor* (*The Literary Man*), and he also began the reprinting of Welsh classics (Gittins 1954). In 1907 Edwards was appointed the Chief Inspector of Education for Wales in the newly created Welsh Department of Education (Jones and Roderick 2003). While some liberals believed the Welsh Department of Education was a pathway to independence, many perceived its creation as a way to mollify Welsh yearnings for self-government. Irrespective of these beliefs, Edwards understood his position as a way to effect what he thought to be beneficial change in the education of the Welsh. As far as Edwards was concerned, his position meant he was to evaluate the needs of education in Wales, sustain the enthusiasm for education there, ensure that the enthusiasm was supported with a system that brought about measurable, positive results, and that the "bilingual problem" in Wales was repositioned as a "bilingual opportunity" (Gittins 1954, p. 89).

In 1907, the Welsh Department of Education put forth its approved syllabus for secondary education noting "the course should provide instruction in the English language and literature, at least one language

other than English, geography, history, mathematics, science, and drawing. Where Welsh is spoken, the language, or one of the languages, other
than English should be Welsh." However, in two short years, Edwards'
influence can be seen in the addendum to this legislation: "any of the
subjects of the curriculum may (whenever local circumstances make it
desirable) be taught partly or wholly in Welsh" (Jones and Roderick
2003, p. 119). As chief inspector, Edwards was successful in organising
a theoretical basis for Welsh medium education in Wales. He was concerned not only with the quality of education, but also about how this
education affected the cultural and political character of the Welsh, and
Wales as a national entity. His is the first developed view of a bilingual
curriculum for Wales, and an educational philosophy that promotes the
inclusion of Welsh interests into a school's curriculum. This was manifest
not only in his appreciation of bilingual schools, but also in encouraging
technical education (which had limited success), and the understanding
that the strengths and needs of a local community should interact with
the processes of education in that community. While many educators
at this time in Wales were interpreting the work of Dewey as child-cen-
tred education, Edwards appreciated a larger understanding of Dewey's
work, one that incorporated the notion that there was an undeniable
relationship between the social and cultural aspects of life in the community and the education of the members of that society (Jones and
Roderick 2003).

Although many people embraced Edwards' enlarged perspective on education, he was not free from controversy. Edwards issued reports attacking
the curriculum put forward by the Central Welsh Board (an entity which he
felt competed with his department) and what he determined to be general
poor teaching. Edwards also engaged in public confrontations with other
educators, particularly the members of the Central Welsh Board. Edwards
was convinced that the introduction of new intermediate schools in Wales
would result in a further dissemination of Anglican influences, influences
he felt were a direct threat to the expression of Welsh culture in schools
in Wales. These conflicts slowed the general development of secondary
schools in Wales and served to weaken Edwards' position in education
with both educators and parents (Jones and Roderick 2003). However,
what could not be undermined was the precedent he established in linking
the viability and relevancy of the Welsh culture in the modern world with
an education that spoke to the distinctiveness of Wales, its culture, and the
needs of its citizens (Jones 1991).

In Reflection

The majority of this work was produced in 2010, and it was my first foray into the educational history of Wales. I was interested in the foundations of Welsh education and the discourses and narratives that helped to establish and define schooling over the centuries. There have been a number of excellent publications regarding the development of educational policy and the impact of devolution on education in Wales (e.g., see Daugherty et al. 2000; Evans 2015), but while those are important, in this chapter, I wanted to examine how earlier themes of citizenship and identity were exercised in establishing schools in Wales. As I look back on this chapter, I am troubled by the subject of philanthropy and its representation here. While the intentions of philanthropy are noble, it would be naive to assume they were exercised with the completely altruistic overtones mentioned above. Those who have the means to act philanthropically obviously had other interests that concerned them. Behind clerics striving to save the souls of the poor and downtrodden were their financial backers who believed the roles of aristocracy and the common folk were divinely appointed. Although these men and women funded schools that ultimately enabled poor children in Wales to read, write, and acquire some skills, they were also concerned with maintaining the divinely inspired social hierarchy and protecting their capital and way of life from those who possessed less but possibly aspired for more.

While the schoolmaster set the curriculum, the church and aristocracy undoubtedly influenced the content of what children learned in school. This is evident in the style of instruction, the lessons presented to boys and to girls, and even in the songs they sang in class. For example, children singing the hymn *All things bright and beautiful* today are missing an important stanza that was regularly sung by children in schools in Wales (and throughout the UK) in the nineteenth century. The stanza reads "The rich man in his castle, the poor man at his gate, God made them high and lowly, and ordered their estate." This simple phrase is a poignant reminder of how those with the means for coordinated educational philanthropy in Wales could influence the curriculum in order to protect their self-interests. Upper class families with the money and means to provide schooling for poor children could also afford to use schooling as a means to reproduce social relations and enforce class distinctions. They could also afford to mobilise narratives and tropes and establish discourses regarding Wales and Welshness. Young people who learned at school and church that they were divinely appointed to be common or low would most likely not question the affluence and position of those designated by God to be affluent. The clergy were not much better. As Christian principles were foundational elements in the formal curriculum of schools in Wales, young people were taught about their relationship with God, the financial and labour-oriented duties of that responsibility, and the need for a holy figure to intercede with God on their behalf.

While modern forms of schooling are no longer as dependent on charitable giving as they once were, philanthropic entities, such as the Bill & Melinda Gates Foundation, continue to influence forms of curriculum and teaching methods in schools throughout the world. In schools today, philanthropy, and religious and political narratives and discourses continue to shape curriculum content, including how pupils and teachers are oriented to discourses of national and cultural identity. In the following chapter, I introduce the Curriculum Cymreig and its role in framing the discourse of citizenship and identity in Wales.

REFERENCES

Bohata, K. (2004). *Postcolonialism revisited: Writing Wales in English.* Cardiff: University of Wales Press.

Daugherty, R., Phillips, R., & Rees, G. (Eds.). (2000). *Education policy making in Wales: Explorations in devolved governance.* Cardiff: University of Wales Press.

Davies, J. (1990). *A history of Wales* (1st ed.). London: Penguin.

Evans, G. (2015). *A class apart: Learning the lessons of education in post-devolution Wales.* Cardiff: Welsh Academic Press.

Gittins, C. (Ed.). (1954). *Pioneers of Welsh education.* Swansea: The Faculty of Education University College.

Gramsci, A. (1971). *Selections from the prison notebooks.* London: Lawrence and Wishart.

Jenkins, D. (1986). *The law of Hywel Dda: Law texts from medieval Wales.* Llandysul: Gomer Press.

Jenkins, G. (2007). *A concise history of Wales.* Cambridge: Cambridge University Press.

Jones, G. (Ed.). (1991). *Education, culture and society.* Cardiff: University of Wales Press.

Jones, G., & Roderick, G. (2003). *A history of education in Wales.* Cardiff: University of Wales Press.

Kreider, J. (2002). "Degraded and Benighted": Gendered constructions of Wales in the Empire, ca. 1847. *North American Journal of Welsh Studies, 2*(1), 24–35.

Lingen, R., Symons, J., & Johnson, V. (1847). *Reports of the commissioners of inquiry into the state of education in Wales, parts I, II, & III*. London: Her Majesty's Stationery Office.

Roberts, G. (1998). *The language of the Blue Books: The perfect instrument of empire*. Cardiff: University of Wales Press.

Shakespeare, W. (2005). King Henry IV. Retrieved August, 2015 from http://shakespeare.mit.edu/1henryiv/full.html

Smith, K. (2007). Resisting the Remnants of English Imperialism: A comparison of African American and Welsh pupils' early 20th century schooling experiences. Unpublished Manuscript. Miami University, Oxford, Ohio, USA.

The National Library of Wales. (2009). Biography of Thomas Gouge. Retrieved August, 2015 from http://yba.llgc.org.uk/en/s-GOUG-THO-1605.html

Williams, J., & Hughes, G. (Eds.). (1978). *The history of education in Wales* (Vol. 1). Swansea: Christopher Davies.

CHAPTER 3

The Curriculum Cymreig

Abstract Smith sheds light into the development of the Curriculum Cymreig. The introduction of this distinctive curricular policy was also accompanied by official guidance for educators in how to successfully plan and implement a Curriculum Cymreig in their schools and classrooms. These considerations were fused together into this new curricular initiative that promised a rising generation of Welsh pupils who not only appreciated a life in Wales, but also recognised Wales' place amongst a global community. Equally important, with the advent of this appreciation and perspective, pupils would hopefully develop a more nuanced and sophisticated understanding of Welshness—of a personalised association with the cultural distinctiveness of Wales and its people.

Keywords Curriculum Cymreig • National Curriculum for wales • Welsh Culture • Welsh Language • Citizenship Education

Vast educational reform would happen relatively quickly in Wales. The influences of the men and women described in Chap. 2 served as catalysts for a series of legislation that led to not only the development of a specific political body to govern education in Wales, but ultimately an environment that would complement the devolution of the Welsh Government. The educational reform acts enacted in the 1940s, and the language recognition acts of the 1960s and 1990s, would ultimately lead to a curricular initiative that intended to reflect a Welsh dimension in learning in Wales.

These acts were motivated by grass-roots movements and political bodies within Wales. With these successes, Welsh control over certain areas of educational development repealed restrictive language legislation that had existed in one form or another since the days of the Tudors. Each of these events signalled a step closer to a chance for devolution. However, the road to devolution was not without its obstacles. The original vote for devolution in 1979 was rejected by the Welsh populace, which kept fixed the majority of educational authority with the bureaucrats in London. Any localised influence was primarily exercised through the Local Education Authorities (LEAs) and county councils. In the 1980s, the conservative movement in Britain peaked with the establishment of Thatcherism and, among other effects, proved to have long-lasting economic ramifications for Wales. This political turn would have devastating effects on the industry-reliant Welsh valleys. Due to Thatcher's determination in controlling the mining unions, the deep-mining coal industry in Wales all but disappeared. Steel mills also closed. Amidst these economic calamities arose an emphasis on the market by Tory governments. Conservative political discourse attacked progressive teaching methods in Wales. It highlighted dilapidated school buildings and outdated technology in the classroom in an effort to add urgency to their claims that Britain's economy and status in the world was under attack. In addition, such arguments claimed that education was the primary method for staving off such advances, and that the conservative movement was what was needed for British pupils to lead the way in saving the British state. What this rhetoric failed to acknowledge was how Thatcherism had undermined the Welsh economy, and, as a result, negatively affected the economic resources available to schools in Wales. The grass-roots movements which supported a bilingual and independent Wales were drowned out by the majority's economic woes. This period in Welsh and English history played a key role in shaping the minds of the Welsh as they looked towards the future of education in Wales. The expansion of powers for the Welsh curriculum authority and the recognition of Cymraeg as an official language in the UK seemed to stem from the work of Welsh educational activists in years prior. If Wales was to continue to play a role in the shaping of its educational future, then the activist tradition of the Welsh, as in the case of Edwards and the Blue Books, would have to be restored.

    In the late 1980s and early 1990s, educational activists and policymakers in Wales developed and implemented a curricular initiative that would have a lasting impact on the nature of education in Wales. While no single charismatic figure emerged as Edwards did in response to the Blue Books of 1847, this fundamental shift in the creation and implementation of a new and distinct curriculum argued for a larger representation of Welsh culture in schools in Wales. The steps taken to make official what was already happening to a lesser degree in certain schools were founded on Edwards' Welsh-centred position of what education, and, in particular, a curriculum of a school in Wales should be.

The Education Reform Act of 1988 signalled a significant shift in educational policy development in England and eventually Wales. Phillips R. (2001) provides an excellent synopsis of how the advent of Thatcherism not only contributed to tumultuous shifts in power relations enacted through competing educational policies and the deterioration of teacher autonomy, but it also potentially provided the political inertia necessary to develop the national curriculum for Wales. The New Right ideology emerging in the late 1980s and early 1990s was a neo-liberal ideology imbued with neo-conservatively charged views privileging discourses of tradition, restoration, and essential elements of cultural and national identity (Whitty 1990). This homogenous view of culture was naturally at odds with cultural relativism and pluralism. Ball (1994) writes that such a perspective views education as a simple enterprise founded on traditions of authority and discipline, relying on the normative nature of nostalgia in promoting a culturally restorative narrative that would shape curriculum development and educational policy in England. Surprisingly, Phillips (2001) purports that the "cultural restorationist strand of New Right ideology may indirectly explain why Wales was granted its own distinctive framework" (p. 101). I echo these comments and, as you will read below, suggest the restorationism present at the time of developing the national curriculum for Wales and Curriculum Cymreig continues to cause tensions within interpretations and implementations of the Curriculum Cymreig today.

In 1993, the Curriculum Council for Wales (CCW) Advisory produced a document entitled *Developing a Curriculum Cymreig*, in which the rationale for this distinctive curriculum and its general characteristics were defined. The guidance suggests the following:

The whole curriculum in Wales encompasses and reflects in its content or exemplification, both the English and Welsh language cultures in the country, and the whole range of historical, social and environmental influences that have shaped contemporary Wales. (CCW 1993)

As mentioned above, the question of a single curriculum for all schools was a relatively new concept which relegated the freedom of teachers to control their curriculum to a phenomenon of the 1960s and 1970s (Jones 1994). As a nationalised curriculum would continue to be developed, the Curriculum Cymreig also continued to undergo further development and revision with updated guidance produced by the ACCAC (Awdurdod Cymwysterau, Cwricwlwm ac Asesu Cymru or Qualifications, Curriculum and Assessment Authority for Wales) in subsequent years. As a result, the Curriculum Cymreig has been redefined and refined to operate within the overall contemporary pedagogical orientation of the educational policies and institutions in Wales. Those developing curriculum for Wales in this period attempted to move past the early, modernistic notions of progress and success—such as Owen's desire for a modern and respectable Wales and his notion of a "true Welsh" identity (Jones and Roderick 2003) without abandoning the romanticised notions of the Gwerin (y 'Werin), or the common folk who existed in the minds of many Welsh. The discourses of cultural restorationism contributing to the distinctive educational policies of education in Wales did not completely dominate educational policies, but neither could it be completely expunged in the name of cultural relativism and pluralism.

In the 1993 and subsequent guidance for teachers, iconic Welsh figures—farmer poets, philosophers, and theologians—continue to exist in various degrees as reliable representations of Welshness in schools and communities throughout Wales. This concept of authentic Welshness was a notion which contributed in part to the curricular perspectives held by Charles and Edwards. However, the most current iteration of the *Developing the Curriculum Cymreig* document is purported to exist within a broader (possibly even somewhat postmodern) discourse, and describes the Curriculum Cymreig as an overarching theoretical perspective incorporated into the national curriculum for Wales that engages multiple interpretations and representations of Welsh cultural and national identity. In many cases, the Curriculum Cymreig has been mistakenly reduced to a policy that simply encourages teachers to reference particular aspects of Wales and Welshness into their courses, and the following statement from the ACCAC document does encourage teachers to thread Welsh themes into their lessons. "To develop such a curriculum, schools should provide and use relevant resources that have a Welsh dimension" (Welsh Government 2003, p. 4). However, although the explicit referencing to Wales and Welshness is a significant portion of the Curriculum Cymreig, the policy is much broader in scope.

A Curriculum Cymreig helps pupils to understand and celebrate the distinctive quality of living and learning in Wales in the twenty-first century, to identify their own sense of Welshness and to feel a heightened sense of belonging to their local community and country. It also helps to foster in pupils an understanding of an outward looking and international Wales, promoting global citizenship and concern for sustainable development. (Welsh Government 2003, p. 4)

As noted above, in addition to developing a sense of association and place with pupils, the Welsh Government purports the Curriculum Cymreig also arms pupils with a sense of global citizenship. This is said to occur through the incorporation of specific references to Wales into the Common Requirements—an aspect of the national curriculum at the time this policy was developed. The Common Requirements consisted of a number of skills and knowledge areas which can be applied to all subjects (Welsh Government 2003). The statement addressing the Common Requirements in the ACCAC document purports that "pupils should be given opportunities, where appropriate, to develop and apply knowledge and understanding of the cultural, economic, environmental, historical and linguistic characteristics of Wales" (Welsh Government 2003, p. 4). Furthermore, without explicitly referring to multicultural education, the guidance frames the implementation of the Curriculum Cymreig as a philosophy that embraces a multicultural approach to education in Wales. For instance, while the original document produced in 1993 discussed only the Welsh and English language cultures, the most current version of the document positions the description of the purpose of the Curriculum Cymreig as a statement that is deliberately inclusive and aims to reflect the plurality and diversity of Wales in the twenty-first century. Its requirements will help pupils to understand what is distinctive about life in Wales, to celebrate diversity, and to acquire a real sense of belonging (Welsh Government 2003, p. 4).

The Welsh Government also identified five dimensions in which the Curriculum Cymreig satisfies the Common Requirements mentioned above. These include cultural, economic, environmental, historical, and linguistic dimensions, and in the document each dimension and its relationship to the Curriculum Cymreig are explored in detail. Aware of the possible misinterpretations of multicultural education, the ACCAC also provides a clear warning:

Because Welsh society is very diverse, there can be no single view of what it is to be Welsh. People's perceptions vary, often coloured by the way of life in their own particular region of Wales, its linguistic, cultural and economic background. Yet all the pupils in our schools share the common experience of living and learning in Wales. They are entitled to have this experience reflected in the school curriculum. Whatever the language of instruction all the five aspects of the Curriculum Cymreig need to be fully developed in all schools. (Welsh Government 2003, p. 7)

The impetus for these elements of the national curriculum for Wales was to be found in the remnants of the national curriculum for England, which had been applied to Wales for decades as a form of curricular template. Over the years, slight adaptations to the curriculum were made, but these adaptations were of more of an interpretive measure than a specific modification of the curriculum itself. These adaptations were born from the same vein of national pride and cultural conservation that were evidenced in the work of Owen and Edwards in years prior. In addition, as with Jones, Charles, Owen, and Edwards, they were also formed through the genuine desire to create in Wales a viable and Sustainable system of education. However, with the development and implementation of the Curriculum Cymreig, Wales has attempted to meet this goal by moving to differentiate its curriculum from the curricula found in other home nations. This differentiation lies in the claim that educators in Wales are encouraged to engage their pupils in a personal identification of Welshness without relying on archaic, stereotypical notions of authentic Welshness. In addition, the Curriculum Cymreig speaks to the desire for educators to enable pupils not only to embrace their own interpretations and understandings of what it means to be Welsh, but also to develop an international perspective and recognition of a global connectedness to other nations and cultures.

This illustrates a willingness for educators in Wales to not only learn from the lessons of the past, but also demonstrate a willingness to utilise developing theories and perspectives in embracing an educational position that strives to meet the needs of all their pupils. Wales continues to establish itself as a viable and capable nation, with many in Wales continuing to work for an independent nation. As such, the role of education as a method of self-improvement and cultural affirmation that has been established by previous educators, and not simply those briefly mentioned in this book, still proves to serve as a meaningful source of personal empowerment that now enjoys a broader theoretical paradigm in Welsh education. However, the developers of the Curriculum Cymreig assert that the Curriculum

Cymreig is intended to not only serve the need for cultural recognition and personal development, but also illustrate the position each pupil possesses in a global community.

Nations have often been described as "imagined communities" (Anderson 1983), meaning they are envisioned, invented, and created as opposed to being fabricated. They are socially constructed and imbued with meaning through discursive practices and performative aspects of language that shape the way we identify ourselves (and others), and generate feelings of association (or disassociation). One of the most potent institutions through which discourses are used to create a nation or sense of national identity are schools. For example, from 1775 to 1783, the American Revolution raged throughout the 13 colonies. As the early colonials entertained the notion of independence, they also illustrated a desire to break away from many of what they regarded were English ideologies and practices. Noah Webster, a pinnacle figure in early American education, wrote, "For America in her infancy to adopt the maxims of the Old World would be to stamp the wrinkles of age upon the bloom of youth" (Kaestle 1983, p. 6). Webster argued for a new language for a new world, "Begin with the infant in his cradle … let the first word he lisps be 'Washington'" (Ibid.). This desire to shape not only the content of an American language but also its form led Webster's "Americanisation" of English words. This "New World" vocabulary was included in textbooks for children in early American schools and served as one of the many means in which the concept of an American nation was constructed through language and promoted through the medium of schooling.

As mentioned in Chap. 2, another example can be found in Welsh history. As a more robust system of schooling began to emerge in Wales in the nineteenth century, the power of schooling as a tool in managing and maintaining cultural identity was also realised. However, instead of using it to build a sense of nationality and belonging, it was intended to reduce difference and aid in cultural assimilation. Through the infamous "Blue Books," Williams demonstrated his belief in the power of schooling in promoting the assimilation of cultural norms and discourses of nation and identity.

In both examples, concepts of citizenship were intrinsically woven into the curricular discourse of schooling. Even in the early stages of public- or state-run schooling, those concerned with nation-building recognised the influence education had over the production of knowledge, representation of culture, and their relationship to producing a coherent narrative for, and concept of, a nation. In both instances above, curriculum and schooling were employed in shaping the character of a culture and nature of a nation, with the first scenario demonstrating resistance against external cultural influences and the second cultural assimilation. In both examples, symbolic and practical action was expressed through curriculum development and implementation in deliberate and organised strategies for building a nation. Nation-building continues in contemporary education, but typically in less ardent terms that stress community, collective association, and political participation. In this regard, CE continues to play a critical role in building and maintaining nation-states and national and cultural identity.

CE IN WALES AND THE CURRICULUM CYMREIG

The Education Reform Act of 1988 brought about the national curriculum of Wales. At the time, educational systems in England and Wales shared many commonalities, and the Education Reform Act of 1988 ensured that, to a degree, those similarities would continue to exist. In addition to the development of a national curriculum closely aligned to that of England, a competing campaign for a separation of English and Welsh approaches to schooling contributed to the development of policies such as *Community and Understanding* and the current *Curriculum Cymreig*, demonstrating the desire for policies to manage the cultural profile of Wales and Welshness. The Curriculum Cymreig continues to be developed, with a review leading to an update being published in 2003. Recommendations from the review suggested the Curriculum Cymreig should be more clearly defined, and 'this new definition be at the core of any future curriculum in Wales' (Welsh Government 2003, p. 11). In 2012, another review of the Curriculum Cymreig took place to determine whether it should continue as a cross-curricular initiative, or whether it would be best implemented through the discipline of history, but, to date, no specific action has yet been taken.

As a cultural initiative within the national curriculum for Wales, the Curriculum Cymreig is intended to promote both a sense of Welshness and belonging as an essential quality of Welsh schools. As mentioned earlier, CE as a curricular subject was introduced to schools in the UK in the early 1990s. In its earliest form, it existed as a cross-curricular theme touching upon multiple specific curriculum subjects, such as History and Geography (Daugherty and Jones 1999). However, it was later endorsed as a statutory subject in England in September 2002 (Watson 2004). In Wales, CE is not a stand-alone subject. Instead, it is delivered as a cross-curricular theme through PSE, ESDGC, and the Welsh Baccalaureate.

Over a decade has passed since the last publication of Developing the Curriculum Cymreig, and schools in Wales have had time to refine, redefine, or even disregard its guidance. A number of studies have investigated relationships between educational initiatives and various social movements and interests in Wales (Jones 2006; Phillips 1996), characterisations of CE in the UK (Arthur et al. 2008), and representations of national identity and diversity among pupils in Wales and in the UK in general (Keating and Benton 2013; Murphy and Laugharne 2011; Scourfield and Davies 2005; Uberoi and Modood 2013; Williams 2003), but there is little in regard to what pupils believe the impact of schooling might have in their orientation to, and association with, cultural and national identity. In the following chapter, I present findings from over seven years of research into the Curriculum Cymreig. These studies are set against my critical discourse analysis of the *Developing the Curriculum Cymreig* document produced by the Welsh Government. The next chapter includes a brief summary of my critical discourse analysis. I then present my work discussing "Welshness" with Year 12 and 13 students in a Sixth Form at a high school in West Wales. Following this discussion, I then present the findings of a study following a cohort of nearly 900 Year 8 and Year 10 pupils. Over the course of three years, these pupils were asked questions derived from *Developing the Curriculum Cymreig* document and other prompts relating to their orientation to Wales and affiliations with Welshness. Finally, I also present conversations I had with primary and secondary teachers, as well as further education instructors, about the Curriculum Cymreig and teaching citizenship and cultural identity in Wales.

REFERENCES

Anderson, B. (1983). *Imagined communities: Reflections on the origins and spread of nationalism.* London: Verso.
Arthur, J., Davies, I., & Hahn, C. (Eds.). (2008). *The SAGE handbook of education for citizenship and democracy.* London: Sage.
Ball, S. (1994). *Education reform: A critical and post structural approach.* Buckingham: Open University Press.
CCW. (1993). *Developing a Cwricwlwm Cymreig.* Cardiff: Curriculum Council for Wales.
Daugherty, R., & Jones, S. (1999). Community, culture and identity: Geography, the National Curriculum and Wales. *The Curriculum Journal, 10*(3), 443–461.

Jones, G. (1994). Which nation's curriculum: the case of Wales. *Curriculum Journal, 5*(1), 5–16.

Jones, G. (2006). Education and nationhood in Wales: An historiographical analysis. *Journal of Educational Administration and History, 38*(3), 263–277.

Jones, G., & Roderick, G. (2003). *A history of education in Wales.* Cardiff: University of Wales Press.

Kaestle, C. (1983). *Pillars of the republic: Common schools and American society, 1760–1860.* New York: Hill and Wang.

Keating, A., & Benton, T. (2013). Creating cohesive citizens in England? Exploring the role of diversity, deprivation and democratic climate at school. *Education, Citizenship and Social Justice, 8*(2), 165–184.

Murphy, A., & Laugharne, J. (2011). Children's perceptions of national identity in Wales. *International Journal of Primary, Elementary and Early Years Education 3–13, 41*(2), 188–201.

Phillips, R. (1996). History teaching, cultural restorationism and national identity in England and Wales. *Curriculum Studies, 4*(3), 385–399.

Phillips, R. (2001). Education, the state and the politics of reform, in R. Phillips and J. Furlong (eds), *Education, Reform and the State: twenty-five years of politics, policy and practice.* London: Routledge/Falmer.

Scourfield, J. B., & Davies, A. (2005). Children's accounts of Wales as racialized and inclusive. *Ethnicities, 5*(1), 83–107.

Uberoi, V., & Modood, T. (2013). Inclusive Britishness: A multiculturalist advance. *Political Studies, 61*(1), 23–41.

Watson, J. (2004). Educating for citizenship: The emerging relationship between religious education and citizenship education. *British Journal of Religious Education, 26*(3), 259–271.

Welsh Government. (2003). Developing the Curriculum Cymreig. Retrieved August 13, 2015 from http://learning.gov.wales/docs/learningwales/publications/130424-developing-the-curriculum-cymreig-en.pdf

Whitty, G. (1990). The new right and the national curriculum: State control or market forces? In B. Moon (Ed.), *New curriculum: National curriculum.* Sevenoaks: Hodder and Stoughton.

Williams, C. (2003). *A tolerant nation? Exploring ethnic diversity in Wales.* Cardiff: University of Wales Press.

CHAPTER 4

Researching Curriculum and Culture in Wales

Abstract Smith summarises a body of research consisting of four studies he conducted related to the Curriculum Cymreig and its role as one of the distinctive elements of schooling in Wales. The studies range from ethnographic projects with students and teachers to a critical analysis of the guidance for teachers for implementing a Curriculum Cymreig, to a longitudinal study involving nearly 900 Year 8 and Year 10 pupils in nearly 30 schools across Wales. The findings suggest the Curriculum Cymreig lacks a sufficient theoretical treatment of culture, and, in particular, Welshness, and the majority of pupils, students, and teachers do not perceive the intended effects of the Curriculum Cymreig in their schooling experience.

Keywords Curriculum Cymreig • Welshness • Welsh Education • National Curriculum for Wales • Welsh Culture

STUDY I: A CRITICAL DISCOURSE ANALYSIS OF THE CURRICULUM CYMREIG

In 2010, I conducted a critical discourse analysis of *Developing the Curriculum Cymreig*. This document was produced by the Welsh Government as a form of guidance for educators in Wales in planning and implementing a Curriculum Cymreig in their schools. In performing this analysis, I was concerned with revealing how the language, formatting, and grammatical features of the text established its authority

© The Editor(s) (if applicable) and The Author(s) 2016   45
K. Smith, *Curriculum, Culture and Citizenship Education in Wales*,
DOI 10.1057/978-1-137-54443-8_4

over the management of Welshness in conjunction with its guidance for the implementation of the Curriculum Cymreig, as well as the ways in which the text represented the concept of Welshness to teachers and pupils. The theoretical framework for this study incorporated the use of critical theory and critical pedagogy, with the method of analysis utilising elements of critical discourse analysis primarily developed by Norman Fairclough (2001).

From this analysis, I determined the text established its authority position through the repeated use of declarative sentences, the foregrounding of quotations from various experts in the field of education, and a combination of relational, experiential, and expressive values in both the language and grammatical features of the text that promoted commonsensical assumptions of the character and quality of "the" or a Welsh identity. In addition, the text possesses a constructivist orientation to Welshness, and promotes this orientation through its emphasis on claims that a "sense of Welshness" can be developed by pupils through learning experiences where they engage in activities possessing a "Welsh dimension," or are conducted in iconic locations in Wales. These activities and locations are described through case studies included in the guidance as a type of shared best practice for how to implement a Curriculum Cymreig in primary and secondary schools. Although the curriculum emerges from a constructivist perspective, the method of identification and association with Welshness that pupils may experience is also nearly a phenomenological practice in that it suggests pupils develop an understanding of Welshness through coming to know the very nature of Welshness, or its most essential value or meaning. In short, pupils are expected to appreciate Wales and develop a sense of Welshness as they discover the intrinsic value of Wales and Welshness through carefully constructed learning experiences that are somehow "exceptionally" Welsh.

In terms of how the text represents Welshness, the guidance regularly highlights the "distinctiveness" of life in Wales, promoting the quality of life as markedly different from that of the other home nations. My analysis produced four themes demonstrating how the text represents the distinctiveness of Wales and Welshness:

- Identifying Welshness through experiencing Traditional Arts
- Identifying Welshness through experiencing Geography
- Identifying Welshness through experiencing History
- Identifying Welshness through experiencing work and play

In concluding my analysis, I believed (and still do) that the Curriculum Cymreig can be an important feature of schooling in Wales. Wales and Welshness, like all cultures, have distinctive features that should be experienced and celebrated. However, how these characteristics are represented, and the ways in which the discourses which mobilise these understandings are legitimised and promoted must also withstand critique. While I believe in culturally appropriate and responsive curricula, I remain sceptical of the aims and objectives of the Curriculum Cymreig, its standards of measurement and evaluation and its claims regarding the impact it has on pupils and teachers. I was curious about pupils' construction of Welshness, what did they think Welshness "is" and what it means to be Welsh? I was also curious as to whether they felt their schooling experience directly affected their appreciation of living in Wales and their ability to develop their own sense of Welshness. Equally important, I was curious as to whether or not teachers felt the Curriculum Cymreig was able to meet the aims set out in the guidance for the curriculum. The following studies are directly related to these concerns. The first is a qualitative investigation of how young people at a high school in mid-Wales describe Welshness and their experience with it. The findings from this study are compared against the conception of Wales and Welshness that underscores the claims presented in *Developing the Curriculum Cymreig*, and reveal interesting parities and fractures between how young people and policymakers come to present Welshness. As mentioned previously, the second study involves pupils' responses to survey questions directly derived from the guidance for the Curriculum Cymreig. The findings continue to demonstrate a disconnect between pupils' experiences and orientations to Wales and Welshness and the assumptions included in *Developing the Curriculum Cymreig*. Following on from those findings, the study then introduces other related longitudinal data that provide a more sophisticated insight into pupils' engagement with Welshness. The third and final study in this chapter presents data from a series of interviews I conducted with Welsh Baccalaureate instructors in local colleges, PSE teachers in secondary schools, and primary teachers. These conversations highlight the teachers' struggles not only in conveying a coherent and well-developed concept of citizenship in Wales, but also in attempting to implement a Curriculum Cymreig in their classes that does not rely on tired tropes of Welshness and cultural artefacts conveying an archaic representation of Wales and Welshness. In each study below, I provide information about the participants, methods, and findings, but rather than discuss the findings for each study individually, I discuss them collectively, framing the data with an approach to identity put forward by Brubaker and Cooper (2000). This is an unconventional approach to discussing the findings of research, but by taking this approach I hope to identify the common themes emerging from each of the studies and emphasise the strengths and weaknesses in how cultural identity is managed through the Curriculum Cymreig.

STUDY II: STUDENTS' PERCEPTIONS OF WELSHNESS

The data for this study were collected through 50 interviews with Year 12 and 13 Sixth Form students at a high school in mid-Wales. The research was an independent project I undertook as part of my doctoral studies and was supported by the Department of Educational Leadership at Miami University in Oxford, Ohio, and the University of Wales Trinity Saint David (UWTSD). In 2008, I was awarded an international teaching and research fellowship for one semester at UWTSD, and it was during my time as a fellow in research that I completed the data collection for this study. Prior to my arrival in Wales, I applied and received ethics approval from Miami University for the research. Once I arrived, I discussed my research with the staff in what is now the School of Social Justice and Inclusion, and we set out a strategy for identifying schools to participate. Although I intended to publish the results of this research at the time, I found my research interests turning more towards the cultural interplay between curriculum and cultural identity and not necessarily pupils' perceptions of cultural identity and the possible effects of schooling. Now, rather than a turn from curriculum to pupils' experiences, my research interests have enabled me to address a number of perspectives on schooling and curriculum, and I feel the data in this research provide a meaningful insight into curricular treatments of Wales and Welshness. While some data may have a "shelf-life," I present these data as a window that shines light into how much, or how little, conversations of culture in schools in Wales have changed over the years.

Several secondary schools across Wales were invited to participate. One school responded indicating that they were interested. This school was located in a rural town in mid-Wales. Although a relatively small and out-of-the-way town, this particular area has a rich cultural, economic, and political history. Additionally, the Welsh language (Cymraeg) continues to feature as an element of the particular kind of Welshness associated with this town and its local surroundings. The school was in its final stages of construction, and it served pupils who previously attended three schools in the local area—two English medium schools and one Welsh medium. Young people in Wales experience a distinctive schooling experience in that bilingualism, even in officially designated "English medium" schools, is a considerable aspect of their daily routine. Cymraeg (the Welsh language) is ever-present in schools in Wales, although to varying degrees of intensity. Although this school was an English medium high school, Cymraeg is frequently spoken by members in the local community. My primary contact with the school was the deputy head teacher, and he was very keen in participating in research that addressed schooling and cultural identity, and, in particular, Welshness.

My decision to interview Sixth Form students was intentional, as I wanted to speak with students who had spent a number of years in primary and secondary education, and now that they were at the end of the compulsory stages of their education, they could reflect on their past and current experiences in talking about schooling and Welshness with me. The deputy head teacher discussed the study with pupils during a morning assembly, and I left informed consent forms for students interested in participating in the study. Over the course of a few days, 65 respondents completed and returned informed consent forms. Out of those 65 students, 50 actually participated in the study. Of those 50 students, 28 were female and 22 were male, and the students were 16 and 17 years of age.

The interview process involved a semi-structured interview schedule which consisted of two broad categories of questions. The first category addressed pupils' understandings of, and orientations to, Welshness and the second category was meant to capture examples and descriptions of how they felt schooling affected their sense of Welshness. The following questions were asked of each of the students:

- If you were to read a definition of Welshness in a dictionary, what do you think it would say?
- How do you define Welshness?
- What does it mean to be Welsh?
- What is it like to be Welsh?
- What learning experiences (both in and out of lessons) have affected your understanding of Welshness?

Often, follow-up questions were asked of students who gave answers that I felt needed further unpacking and investigation. These questions often revealed complex and nuanced descriptions of students' experiences and provided them with the opportunity to reflect upon and analyse their responses. Initially, the interviews were conducted over a course of four months. I met with the students in a small room adjacent to the annex where they would spend their free lessons. During the weeks working with these young people, I regularly reflected on my experiences interviewing the students by keeping a field journal. I would ruminate on their responses and consider my own assumptions and representations of Welshness, and my participation in collecting data from these students. The interviews were recorded and later transcribed. In many cases, the responses were transcribed verbatim, and when this was not possible or necessary, summary statements encapsulating the students' response were recorded.

Methods of thematic and content analysis were used in analysing the students' responses. I listened to the interviews a number of times to familiarise myself with the data. I reviewed my field journal as I listened to the recordings and compared my notes regarding the experience of collecting data to what I at the time had identified as important excerpts from the interviews. Eventually, I began to organise the data by question, identifying each response by pupil. The number of interviews I collected created a large set of data, so I reduced the number of interviews I would analyse from 50 to 20. This was initially accomplished through random assignment, but after appraising the data and respondents, I altered the sample to ensure it included a diversity of respondents. The final 20 interviews included both male and female respondents, students who identified as Welsh, "not Welsh," or did not really know how to identify themselves culturally, and ethnically diverse students. The sample also included students who demonstrated a variety of fluency in Welsh, with some students having been primarily raised as first language Welsh speakers to pupils who only studied Cymraeg at school until Year 10. I then organised responses within themes emerging from the data, as well as candidate themes for further organisation and analysis. I also gave heed to the number of times key phrases and words were used in conjunction with concepts of Welshness, but I used this primarily as an organisational device and do not report the frequency of these phrases for the basis of any of the claims in this research.

The final stages of analysis included recognising theme patterns and discursive formations within those patterns that lent to the construction of a narrative of Welshness and pupils' experiences with schooling and cultural identity. This process resulted in a contextualised and meaningful exploration into the students' orientation to Welshness and their schooling experiences. Once this stage of the analysis was complete, I made arrangements with the deputy head teacher to discuss the results with the 20 interviewees. Unfortunately, only five of the students were available to review the results. I asked if there were any items they wanted changed, clarified, or reviewed again, but they indicated they were pleased with the results.

As mentioned previously, the data were collected and initially analysed in 2008. In considering what I would discuss in this book, I decided to revisit these data to see if they were still relevant to discussions of schooling and cultural identity. I listened to the interviews again, with the advantage of seven years of scholarship to inform my reintroduction to these students' and their views. I read my field journal and the final analysis, making additional notes and comments where necessary. This process of revisiting the past, yet realising many of the questions I was seeking to answer are still with me today, gave me confidence in the relevance of the data and their importance in better understanding how we teach citizenship and culture in schools in Wales today.

Many of the limitations I faced in this study were due to students' school schedules. I was cognisant of the fact that these pupils were giving up a free lesson to speak with me about Welshness and schooling when they could have spent time revising or even just taking a break between lessons with their friends. I was also mindful of the fact that I was a guest in the school, and that my presence there could possibly cause unintentional disruptions. I could have spent far more time with the students, and would have benefitted from multiple interviews or even possibly focus groups where they could feed off of the synergy that arises through guided discussion. Additionally, it would have been beneficial to speak with teachers about their experiences in the classroom and their responses to some of the remarks made by the students. In-class observations would have also provided another dimension of analysis set between the claims of teachers and students regarding how Welshness is conveyed through schooling in this quiet rural town. Unfortunately, these opportunities were outside of the scope for the project at the time, but the current data set is situated well within the other studies presented in this book, and I believe they add a necessary and poignant perspective on pupils' engagement with cultural identity and citizenship in schools in Wales.

Defining Welshness

I asked the students to give me a "textbook definition" of Welshness because I wanted them to think about how others might define it, but not just any definition; I wanted it to feel like an "official" definition. Students often use dictionaries as an official definitive resource for the meaning of words. They rely on these books, often without questioning how or why the words in the dictionary are defined the way they are. This is the kind of response I was hoping to get from the students, an almost assumed, common-sense definition. I felt this would tell me a lot about what discourses were at play in the representation of Welshness they had experienced so far. I could not know if school, family, or other institutions were contributing to these discourses—it was likely that all of these institutions contributed, to some degree, to the way in which these students would define it, but that was not important. What was important in asking this question was the ways in which the students would attempt to define Welshness. Would it be easy? Would they struggle? Would they rely on well-exercised, traditional accounts, or would they depart from traditional discourses and give a particular and distinctive insight?

Throughout the course of the interviews, the students struggled with articulating a "textbook definition" of Welshness. Over half of the students initially started their response with "I don't know," which could have been a strategy for buying time while they thought about the answer, but it felt more than that. Many were flabbergasted, confronted with the task of doing something they had never done before—define something that was presented to them as an already defined concept. This was something that, particularly in school, existed to these students as an a priori concept. When some students could finally put something together, they usually relied on traditional, almost stereotypical definitions. Nearly every pupil mentioned Cymraeg, although many of them did not speak Welsh fluently. They also mentioned patriotism and pride in the country. The majority of students said someone had to be born in Wales, or living in Wales to be "Welsh," even though they moved to Wales at a very young age. These were not unexpected responses and were the easiest elements of Welshness, the most readily available aspects of an "official definition" that the students could recollect, but I was interested in much more than that.

Many of the responses were similar to that of Nia, a Year 12 female student, who was born in the area and attended schools there all her life. She simply said, "I don't know. Someone who spoke the language probably, or lived here." I asked her to tell me more about what she meant, but she had difficulty not repeating the same ideas, just worded differently. Other students varied on Nia's theme and included ideas such as "having a strong accent," "being patriotic," and "supporting Wales in rugby." Ioan, a Welsh-speaking, Year 13 male student, clearly demonstrated the difficulty he had in defining Welshness when, after running through the same old routine of language, "born there" and rugby, he said "It's impossible to sum up really, the words just don't come to mind."

After the students attempted their "textbook definitions" of Welshness, I wanted to know more about their own understanding of it. I asked them how they would define it in their own words. Based on their own perspective and experiences, I wanted to know how they come to define Welshness. Unsurprisingly, the definitions did not change much. Again, the students struggled. "I don't know!" Came one reply from Sylvia, an animated and talkative Year 12 female student. "It's hard! We never talk about what Welshness is, we all just sort of think we know!" Similar responses to the textbook definition were initially provided by many of the students. Things like "the Welsh language," "being born or living in Wales," having "pride in Wales," and "knowing the history or culture" of Wales were typical responses. I kept pushing, asking them to elaborate on these ideas and to tell me more about it from their perspective. Soon, we were back into the "I don't know!" responses, but after all the "I don't know" and "this is hard" responses were depleted, the students started to think more carefully about Welshness and how they come to define it.

Cymraeg as Welshness

Speaking Welsh was a common theme across all of the answers. All the students mentioned Welsh, but they had varying opinions about how it contributed to Welshness. Diane, a self-identified, semi-fluent Welsh speaker said, "The language makes Wales different, but you don't have to speak the language to feel Welsh, you just have to know that Wales has its own language." Other pupils mentioned the importance of speaking Welsh. Dafydd, a Year 13 male student, who strongly identified as a farmer said, "Welshness means you speak Welsh, it's important that we speak Welsh because that's an important part of Welsh culture, if you don't speak Welsh it will die and Welsh culture will die too."

Family and Community Traditions

A number of students referenced a knowledge of Welsh culture and participation in Welsh traditions. When I asked them to define Welsh culture, they immediately referenced activities like the Urdd and Eisteddfod, performance events that included singing, dancing, and recitation exclusively through the medium of Welsh. The students primarily engage in these activities through the school. Some students stated that supporting Wales in rugby and eating cawl (a traditional Welsh stew) were important elements of Welsh culture, and were the most readily available examples of Welshness. For them, Welshness was directly tied to participating in these events, but they did not describe how or why this participation was typically Welsh. However, Buddug, a Year 12 female student studying drama, was an exception. She said,

> "I think you have to engage in the culture, you have to know and participate in the traditions—things like eating cowl, or maybe farming, those kinds of things that we understand as being Welsh, but everybody eats soup, and people farm all over the place, so it's knowing that you're doing it here, in a way that's been handed down over the years and by ways that other people here are doing it that make it 'Welsh,' so that's what I think Welshness is, it's doing things in a way that somehow tell you you're Welsh."

What Buddug understood was the simple the act of supporting Wales or eating cawl did not make one Welsh, but that there was something associated with those activities, with the meaning one derives from these activities, that helped one feel more associated with Wales and Welsh culture. Thomas, a Year 12 male pupil, who was a big history buff provided a similar sentiment, but added an important distinction; he said,

> "I think it's wanting to be part of something, wanting to feel like you're different from something else. Like in Wales, we want to be understood as being different from English, so we do things that make us feel Welsh, but also show other people that we're Welsh. I don't mean different in a way that makes other places, like England seem bad (although that sometimes happens), but that we're not the same, there is something different about Wales—we have a different language, a different history and those things help makes us who we are. Those who say they're Welsh feel that the things that make Wales different from England (for example) are the things they want to be known by, so they do things to feel Welshness and to show their Welshness."

WHAT DOES IT MEAN TO BE WELSH?

This was a difficult question for the students to answer, but it is a question that was derived from their responses. It was clear that as the students thought more carefully about the definition of Welshness, they came to understand that the qualities of Welshness were derived from the meanings conveyed through social and cultural interaction. Without delving too deeply into constructivism or symbolic interactionism, it is clear these pupils were suggesting that the values and notions of Welshness were conveyed through the meanings people apply to the activities they described as being Welsh, so I was interested in the values of those meanings. I was interested in trying to understand what is meant when someone says "I'm Welsh."

We ran through the typical "I don't know" responses until I was able to repeatedly rephrase the question in order to help the pupils unpack its purpose. What I learned from this interaction can be categorised into two themes: "association" and "the unacknowledged." Through drilling down into the purpose of the question, the majority of pupils said Welshness meant that a person wanted to be associated with a concept of Wales that was (a) presented to them, (b) constructed by them, or (c) a little bit of both. They said that a person who says they are Welsh is consciously associating themselves with other people who identify as Welsh. They also said they felt these people were associating themselves with the country, its history, and culture. Gareth, an affable Year 13 student, with a Y Ddraig Goch (the Welsh Red Dragon) tattoo said, "It means I'm part of something, something that has lasted a long time, it has a history and a heritage that I'm proud of. I'm proud to be Welsh. It means a lot to me." Being "a part of something" was a concept that ran through many of the students' responses. Community is key. When discussing Welshness, many of the students struggled to define Welshness; they told anecdotes of friendliness and support from members in their community as a means to convey their understanding of Welshness. For them, Welshness was a particular form of associated living. It involved people living together, being involved, and knowing and looking out for each other. In speaking of it in these terms, the students realised it was "kind of a big deal" and some were taken back by the scope of what it means when you make a statement regarding your cultural identity, but they also recognised the fluidity of that association. "It means you want to be a part of something," one student said, "but that feeling can change over time. I felt it much stronger when I was in primary school than I do now."

The other theme, "the unacknowledged," refers to the majority of responses I received from the students. Time after time, when the students were struggling to convey what it meant to be Welsh, they would say things like "I don't know what Welshness means, I guess I only know what it is. We never talk about what it means." Dafydd said his Welsh teacher would talk about being Welsh, but as a class they

> "never really took time to think about what that meant when we said 'I'm Welsh.' I think we all just assumed it meant we were from Wales, but now that I think of it, it can mean a lot of different things. It's still Welshness, but the meaning of Welshness from a person in Caernarvon can be really different from the difference of someone in Swansea. Welshness can be so diverse, but it gets summed up somehow into this insignificant word."

WHAT'S IT LIKE TO BE WELSH?

"It's LUSH!" came one response from Sylvia. She smiled a big cheesy grin as she continued. "Wales is beautiful, and different, it's so small and no one really knows anything about us. When I go abroad, people say 'where you from' and I say 'Wales,' and they go 'where is that? Is that England?' and then I get to tell them all of the great things about being Welsh." Overall, the majority of students I spoke to enjoyed being Welsh. They felt distinctive, set apart. They felt Wales has a particular history and identity that is discrete from the cultural and historical profiles of the other home nations. "Being Welsh," mused Buddug, "is great because we have the Welsh language, and we have this great history and we have a lot of people who have become celebrities and singers, it makes you feel good!"

However, even positive associations can be tempered by the less positive aspects of living in Wales. In describing what it's like to be Welsh, Dafydd revealed some of the conflict he experiences.

> "It's weird, you live in Wales your whole life and you slag it off, but when you meet people outside of Wales, we love it. The weather is awful, miserable—but for some reason we love it. We have the breath-taking places, but they're everywhere you look so you get used to it, but when people ask you about what you think about Wales, I say I hate it. To me, it's just sort of who I am. I love it, but I hate it."

LEARNING EXPERIENCES AND WELSHNESS

I asked each student what learning experiences at school helped them better understand Welshness. In many ways, this seemed an easier question to answer. The most common response referred to their Welsh lesson.

Welsh as a second language is a compulsory subject at schools in Wales, and the students often mentioned how their teachers demonstrated a passion and interest in "all things Welsh." Kathryn, a Year 12 female student, said, "Welshness is talked about a lot in Welsh lessons, and things like S4C, the Urdd, Eisteddfod and stuff like that. My Welsh teacher last year used to tell us all of the great places to visit in Wales." Other students also mentioned Welsh lessons, but they focused on how learning Welsh helped them engage in Welshness. For example, Ioan said, "I learned the language at school, and I think that helped. Knowing the language makes you feel like you know more about the country, but as far as actual information about the history or culture of my country, I don't really know."

Other students were less convinced that school impacted their sense of Welshness. For example, Aimee, a Year 13 student, who wants to be a veterinarian said,

"Welshness isn't something we really talk about that much. At school we have eisteddfod and St David's Day, and that's about it really. There's nothing really in doing apart from the occasional assembly, because they might speak Welsh here and there, but that's about it really." In fact, apart from the occasional connection to Welshness in their Welsh lessons, most pupils did not think school was a place where they learned about Welsh history or culture, not to mention Welshness. Many pupils felt they did not really know the history of Wales or what made Welsh culture particularly Welsh. Mary, a Welsh-speaking, Year 13 student, said she felt she lost "some of my vocabulary because I can't use my full range of Welsh language here. You sort of lose out on speaking Welsh at this school, and as far as Welsh culture and history, you learn about Welsh poetry and singers in Advanced Subsidiary (AS) levels, and Welsh heroes, but that's about it." I asked her how she felt about those lessons where she learned about Welsh history and she said, "It's nice to hear about the past, because I didn't know anything about Welsh history before coming to this school."

While Mary enjoyed her experience learning about Welsh history and culture, other students felt their understanding of and orientation to Welshness had waned since attending secondary school. In speaking to this point, Gareth said,

"Primary school helped me more than secondary school. In primary school, they encouraged me to speak Welsh, and to get involved in things like St David's Day. It was bigger there. On the playground, your friends would encourage you to speak Welsh, but not here. The Eisteddfod helps here, but that's about it really. There's Welsh class, so they tell you what Wales and Welshness is, but we don't really get to learn it for ourselves."

Sylvia echoes Gareth's comments, adding,

"At Welsh lesson you hear about Welsh nationalists and rebels and stuff like that—I've never heard of it before, and it's interesting at first, but when it's rammed down your throat it's not. When they go on too much about it, or make you feel guilty for not knowing things, then I don't like it. They don't really give us a chance to talk about it, they just tell it to us and expect us to care."

As I worked with these students, I felt they were genuinely interested in talking about culture and identity. Many of them remarked that they did not have these discussions in their lessons and did not have opportunities to think about the nature of culture, its role in society, and how it impacts our self-concept and interaction with others. As noted above, I will collectively discuss the findings of this research with the information from the other studies. However, both the ways in which the pupils discussed Welshness and their desire for more meaningful discussions of Welshness, culture, and cultural identity in general were important factors in shaping how I would examine the Curriculum Cymreig in my later research. In the following study, I build on these students' responses and try to understand the ways in which Year 8 and Year 10 pupils feel schooling has affected their appreciation for Wales and their ability to develop their own sense of Welshness.

STUDY III: LEARNING WELSHNESS

In 2013, as part of a research team at the Wales Institute of Social & Economic Research Data & Methods (WISERD) at Cardiff University, I surveyed 849 pupils aged 12–15 in schools across Wales. These pupils were asked a number of questions covering a wide array of topics relating to their experience of living and learning in Wales. Of importance to this research were questions relating to their orientation to, and affiliation with, Wales and Welshness. In 2014, a second sweep of data collection was undertaken. During this sweep, we asked pupils questions related to their appreciation of and affiliation with Wales. As is typical with longitudinal studies, some of the original respondents were not able to participate in this sweep, and new participants consented to join. In 2015, a third sweep of data collection was conducted, and, as before, some pupils who had previously participated were not available and some new pupils decided to participate.

Each series of findings presented below will describe who participated and when. For example, findings presented from the second and third sweeps will specifically state if the results provided were based on pupils participating in single or multiple sweeps. If multiple responses are provided, the description accompanying the findings will indicate if the responses provided in Sweeps 2 or 3 were provided by the same pupil in an earlier sweep. In addition to the data collected in these sweeps, I conducted interviews with head teachers during the first sweep. The purpose of the interviews was to gain an insight into the ways in which head teachers understood and implemented the Curriculum Cymreig in their schools, and they provide a fascinating glimpse at the contrast between the intent and language of the curriculum from a policy perspective and the actual interpretation and implementation by head teachers and their staff. Additionally, the findings of the research are provided below by sweep. The first sweep focuses on questions derived from the *Developing the Curriculum Cymreig* document. The second sweep introduces questions about living in Wales as an adult, and the third sweep repeats the questions of Sweeps 1 and 2, and also introduces new questions of "feeling at home" and "feeling Welsh" in Wales.

Sweep 1: The Curriculum Cymreig and Pupils

Each of the young people was asked how much they agreed with the followings statements: (a) schools helps me appreciate living in Wales and (b) school helps me develop my own sense of Welshness. These statements may seem familiar as they are two of the primary aims of the Curriculum Cymreig. In a way, I was testing the ability of the Curriculum Cymreig to obtain the goals set out in the curricular guidance. Additionally, I wanted to know if pupils could notice specific interventions in the development of their appreciation of Wales or their sense of Welshness. Once the data were collected, I then interviewed the head teachers for a number of the schools in the study. Although I wanted to know how they and their teachers might implement the Curriculum Cymreig, I was primarily concerned with how they might attempt to meet the aims and goals of the curriculum through the schooling activities.

The results of the student survey show a possible relationship between the pupils' perception of the impact of the Curriculum Cymreig and their advancement through school. Of the 838 participants in Sweep 1, 325 (38.8%) agreed school helped them appreciate living in Wales and 319 (38.1%) agreed school helped them develop their own sense of Welshness. When the pupils' responses were organised by year, the Year 8 pupils were more likely to agree to these statements than the Year 10 pupils. For example, 188 (45.7%) of the Year 8 pupils agreed school helped them appreciate living in Wales compared to 138 (32.3%) of the Year 10 pupils. The results were almost the same for the statement about school helping them develop their own sense of Welshness, with 43.3% of the Year 8 pupils and only 33.2% of the Year 10 pupils agreeing.

In regard to national identity, the children who were most likely to agree that school helped them develop their own sense of Welshness were pupils who already described themselves as being Welsh (43.1%) and the pupils who were least likely to agree were those who self-identified as English (27.4%). Young people who identified themselves as British were the group most likely to disagree (31.3%).

The pupils were also asked how well they could speak Welsh and these results were organised into four categories: (a) I speak Welsh fluently, (b) I can speak a lot in Welsh, but not fluently, (c) I can speak a few words and phrases in Welsh, and (d) I cannot speak Welsh. Because fluency can be a difficult concept to measure, these categories were organised into two broad codes—more fluent and less fluent. Interestingly, nearly half (49.2%) of the "more fluent" pupils agree schooling helped them develop their own sense of Welshness compared to only 25.5% of the "less fluent" pupils.

Finally, given the concerns the *Developing the Curriculum Cymreig* document places over Welshness being an accessible and inclusive identity that accommodates a diverse spectrum of ethnic and cultural backgrounds, I was interested to know how minority pupils might feel about school and its impact on their appreciation of Wales and sense of Welshness. In order to do this, the young people were asked to indicate which ethnicity best described them: white, Asian, black, Mixed, or Other. In order to conduct a reliable analysis, the Mixed, Asian, black, and Other groups were combined into one category called BME, meaning British Minority Ethnicity; 752 (88.6%) of the pupils identified as white and 97 (11.4%) identified as BME. The most interesting result in regard to pupils' ethnicity is the percentage of pupils who disagree that school helps them develop their own sense of Welshness. While only 165 (22.3%) of the white students disagree, 37 (38.1%) of the BME students also disagree with the statement. These data suggest a clear cause for concern regarding the purported inclusivity of the Curriculum Cymreig and its ability to engender within pupils, and especially BME pupils, an appreciation for Wales and their own sense of Welshness—both of the variables play into a much larger concern regarding these pupils' sense of belonging in school and in Wales overall.

In addition to the Curriculum Cymreig statements, we wanted to know if pupils felt like they would live in Wales as adults. I refer to these survey items as the Living in Wales questions. These statements help us to potentially understand how pupils value living in Wales as adult. Of the 833 responses, only 165 (19.8%) said they would "definitely" live in Wales when they were older. We followed up this statement with another asking them if, when they were older, they would live in the same area as they do now. Of the 830 responses, only 41 (4.9%) said they would "definitely" live in the same area as they do now.

In interviews with the head teachers, each head teacher said their school had a formal Curriculum Cymreig policy. When asked how well the policy was implemented in their school, the majority of head teachers believed their school implemented a Curriculum Cymreig well, with a minority suggesting their implementation could be improved. Overwhelmingly, the rationale head teachers used in describing the success of their Curriculum Cymreig was primarily dependent on the use of the Welsh language at school. For example, in the following passage, a head teacher in rural mid-Wales describes how his school implements a Curriculum Cymreig:

> We have ten incidental Welsh words and we are trying to get staff up to 20. We have English speaking teachers who will always put "gwaith dosbarth" (class work) and the month in class, and they use Welsh stampers like "da iawn" (very good). It's at that level really, we have bilingual assemblies, we have Welsh medium in school and that helps, Welsh language tutoring groups.

A head teacher in a coastal area of mid-Wales indicated that although the school has a Curriculum Cymreig policy, it needed improvement. Like the head teacher above, his interpretation of a healthy Curriculum Cymreig, and indeed, a Welsh ethos, is entirely dependent on language use:

> It's something we need to work on, our Welsh ethos. Many pupils feel Welsh is less important and… some pupils enjoy Welsh. About 50 of our pupils are Welsh first language standard. So what we are doing next September is to introduce more Welsh Medium teaching.

He continued to describe what he felt was the character of the school in terms of the Welsh language and how that disposition affects the implementation of a Curriculum Cymreig:

It's not the badge that we wear. In none of the terms I used to discuss this school did I say bilingual. If you went to other schools in this area, they would talk about bilingualism. We could do more, but are kind of naturally, what we are. The nature of the school is a natural expression of the adults and the children that are in this school, and the nice thing about that is there is no politics at all whatsoever, it doesn't matter who can/can't speak Welsh, where they come from, how many generations have been in Wales, none of those things are coming through at all.

Like all the secondary schools in this study, the Curriculum Cymreig is only understood as a language policy, and in this particular school the attitudes towards Welsh language use minimalise the degree to which a Curriculum Cymreig can be enacted. When asked about addressing Welsh culture rather than simply Welsh language, the head teacher began to address cultural observances in the school, but his response rapidly strayed from the topic of Cymreig (Welsh culture) back to Cymraeg:

We celebrate St David's day. We do more with Welsh Medium assemblies and Welsh Medium registrations, but I'm not in the game of forcing anyone to speak Welsh. You just have to encourage it and explain why it's important for them to keep those skills.

Another head teacher at rural mid-Wales near the English border demonstrates a broader understanding of the Curriculum Cymreig by saying, "It's not just the language issue, I think being Welsh is more than about the language, it's about the identity." However, when asked how his school enacts a Curriculum Cymreig, he also emphasises Welsh language use:

The pupils always write the date in Welsh. There is Welsh written in every lesson, it's small, but everybody does it. It's in the pupils' planner.

It is clear that tensions exist within schools at the intersection of curriculum and culture, but also at the convergence of national policy and local practice. In schools in Wales, those tensions emerge from a variety of sources such as traditional uses and attitudes towards the Welsh language, themes of nationalism and the conceptualisation and implementation at both the national and local scale of Welsh educational policy. For example, the head teacher of the rural school near the English border describes the tensions arising from ESTYN inspections and teachers' attitudes towards implementing a Curriculum Cymreig:

It's the big criticism of the inspectors—the argument about consistency of staff who do it enthusiastic and lovingly, staff who do it begrudgingly and some choose to ignore it. And then, of course, if they ignore it and are told to do it, they do it begrudgingly and the possibly minimum.

In the ESTYN inspection reports for the schools in this study, references to a Curriculum Cymreig were made, comprising language similar to that of the head teachers. Welsh language use was emphasised over a Welsh culture or ethos (although some references to these concepts were mentioned). In regard to primary schools, inspection reports were more likely to mention Welsh culture, but the language of the inspectors was primarily concerned with Welsh language use. The responses of head teachers at the primary schools in our study were also concerned with Welsh language use, but they expanded their interpretation of the Curriculum Cymreig to include learning experiences that acknowledged Welsh culture within the school and community, as well as a desire to create and promote a Welsh ethos. For example, a head teacher at a primary school in the South-Eastern valleys described the enactment of a Curriculum Cymreig at her school in regard to both Welsh language and ethos:

> We are really lucky in this school because a lot of our staff have a really good knowledge of Welsh as a second language. We also have third party support for Welsh language. We also have a strong Welsh ethos here. Our year 5 children are studying "black gold," they're doing lots of things with mining, etc.

The "black gold" studied by Year 5 pupils is of course coal, and in this valley school the curriculum tapped into local histories and traditions involving the legacy of mining. During the time this interview was held, a number of local communities were observing the commemoration of a major mining disaster, and the pupils from this school were involved in research projects, performances, and visits to historical sites on mining in the valleys as part of that observation. The head teacher of a primary school in mid-Wales also discussed a Welsh ethos in his description of the Curriculum Cymreig activities at his school:

> In the past, there has not been a huge focus on Welsh and the Curriculum Cymreig within the school, it's been there and they've paid lip service to it.

So, it's a case now of trying to lift that. A Welsh ethos is not accessible to the extent that I would like to see. You can't talk about Welsh culture without first talking about the Eisteddfod, we held our first one last year—there had never been a school eisteddfod prior to that; so many wanted to take part that it took all day.

The head teacher of a primary school in a coastal area of mid-Wales described the Curriculum Cymreig at his school as

an attitude that is taught through all the subjects. Yes, it's being aware, both consciously and subconsciously, that we are a school in Wales and a Welsh community—I say that as someone who is not Welsh, but the children understand that. This is where we are, this is the community in which we are, this is a community school and therefore we must meet the needs of this community—the global community as well, but first this community.

In Cardiff, a head teacher of a primary school with a multiculturally diverse population responded that I'm confident that every aspect of the Curriculum will have a Welsh take on it. I'm passionate about living in Cardiff and taking our children out and about. It's the capital city of Wales and it's got fantastic facilities for all citizens—not just a few, and many of our children wouldn't have the opportunity to go to Y Senydd (Senate) or Millennium Centre if it wasn't for school. In this study, less than 40 % of the pupils surveyed believed schooling positively impacted their orientation to Wales and Welshness. The interpretation of the Curriculum Cymreig policy by primary and secondary schools in this study can provide an insight as to why so few pupils feel that schooling helps them appreciate Wales and develop their own sense of Welshness. While Welsh language use was regularly mentioned in school documents and interviews, primary schools were more likely to display Welsh flags, red dragons, daffodils, and other traditional representations of Welsh culture. These activities can be interpreted as tokenistic appeals to an "authentic" Welshness, but they also demonstrate a consideration of Welshness outside the limits of Welsh language use, incorporating simple representations of Welshness for young pupils in an attempt to create an atmosphere of Welshness that can nourish a sense of place with pupils. The secondary schools typically had less representations of Welshness, with the most common item on display being the Welsh flag.

Sweep 2: Living and Feeling at Home in Wales

In 2014, the WISERD team revisited the pupils participating in the study. No head teachers were interviewed during this sweep. While the results described in Sweep 1 include responses from Year 8 and Year 10 pupils, only the Year 8 cohort were surveyed in later sweeps. The survey covered a number of themes, but the statements relevant to this research are the following: (a) If I could live anywhere in the world, I would live in Wales, (b) I feel Wales is my real home, and (c) I live in Wales, but I do not feel particularly Welsh. I refer to these statements in this research as the Home statements. The responses the pupils could choose from were "Strongly agree," "Agree," "Neither agree nor disagree," "Disagree," and "Strongly disagree." For the purpose of analysis and comparison to other sweeps, these categories were collapsed into "Agree," "Neither agree nor disagree," and "Disagree." Of the 368 pupils (now in Year 9) in Sweep 2, 314 had also participated in the first sweep. I was most interested in their results because I wanted to see if there was any suggestion of a potential relationship between their answers to the Curriculum Cymreig statements in Sweep 1 and the Home statements in Sweep 2 (Table 4.1).

With these findings in mind, I wanted to know if pupils who agreed or disagreed with the Curriculum Cymreig statements gave similar responses to the Home statements. To do this, I compared the responses of pupils in Sweep 1 to their responses to the Home statements of Sweep 2. The first comparison is between pupils' responses to "school helps me appreciate living in Wales" and "If I could live anywhere in the world, I would live in Wales." Of the pupils who say school helps them appreciate living in Wales, only 33 (32.7%) would choose to live in Wales from any location in the world. In regard to Wales being their "real home," 55 (51.9%) of the pupils who agree also say school helps them appreciate living in Wales. Nationality also seems to have an effect on the ways in which pupils feel

Table 4.1   Living and feeling at home in Wales

	Agree	Neither agree nor disagree	Disagree
If I could live anywhere in the world, I would live in Wales (*n*=313)	92 (29.4%)	92 (29.4%)	129 (41.2%)
I feel Wales is my real home (*n*=314)	202 (64.3%)	65 (20.7%)	47 (15%)
I live in Wales, but I don't particularly feel Welsh (*n*=314)	106 (33.8%)	55 (17%)	153 (48.8%)

at home in Wales. For example, while 67 (63.8%) of the pupils identifying as Welsh feel Wales is their "real home," only 8 (27.6%) of English pupils feel the same. Additionally, pupils who are most likely to disagree with this statement are English pupils, with 6 (20.7%) saying they did not feel like Wales was their "real home."

In regard to schooling helping pupils develop their sense of Welshness and its potential relationship to their sense of Wales being their "real home," there was no significant statistical relationship to suggest that one variable had an impact on the other. The same holds true for the relationship between schooling developing their sense of Welshness and them living in Wales but not particularly feeling Welsh. However, there are other factors that seem to play a role in affecting how pupils responded to our Sweep 2 statements. For example, we know the ethnicity of the majority of the pupils participating in the study. Of the 193 pupils whom have identified with a particular ethnicity and participated in both sweeps, we see important differences in how white and BME pupils respond to the statement, "If I could live anywhere in the world, I would live in Wales." Of the 193 white pupils responding to this statement, 55 (28.9%) compared to 1 (4.5%) of the BME pupils agreed.

Sweep 3: Revisiting the Curriculum Cymreig in School

In Sweep 3, we repeated questions from Sweeps 1 and 2 to determine if any changes over time had occurred among our sample. At Sweep 3, our pupils were now in Year 10. This is an important year as it marks the beginning of studying for the GCSE exams and preparations for exiting compulsory schooling in the following year. In the following section I present longitudinal data regarding the Curriculum Cymreig statements and Living in Wales questions of Sweep 1. Of the 313 pupils who answered the questions discussed in this research in Sweeps 1 and 2, 232 also participated in Sweep 3, and their responses are provided in Table 4.2.

As shown in Table 4.2, there is a significant change in pupils' perceptions of the impact of schooling on their appreciation of living in Wales and the development of their own sense of Welshness. Not only did less pupils in Sweep 3 agree with these statements compared to the first sweep, but more pupils also disagreed. The number of pupils who were ambivalent in Sweep 1 also decreased in Sweep 3, suggesting that pupils who once agreed or at least did not disagree with the statements came to a new understanding regarding their appraisal of the impact of schooling and their affiliation with Wales and Welshness. These data may reflect a growing sense of pessimism towards school as the pupils advance in their studies. However, assuming pupils' maturity and overall development as they progress through school, these data may more appropriately suggest that these young people are thinking more critically about how schooling affects these dimensions of their lives and identity. Moreover, these data also suggest that the Curriculum Cymreig and its implementation in schools may not be an effective way to promote Wales or Welshness among young people, or that it engenders feelings of positive association or identity development among young people at school (Table 4.3).

In regard to the Living in Wales questions, a shift similar to the Curriculum Cymreig statements occurs as pupils progress from Year 8 to Year 10. By Year 10, these respondents were far more likely to disagree with these questions than in Year 8. What is difficult to know is the reason why this shift took place. For example, as these pupils mature and begin to think more seriously about what they want to achieve in life, their

Table 4.2 Longitudinal analysis—Curriculum Cymreig statements

	Sweep 1 (n = 228)			Sweep 3 (n = 227)		
	Agree	Neither agree nor disagree	Disagree	Agree	Neither agree nor disagree	Disagree
School helps me appreciate living in Wales	109 (47.8 %)	77 (33.8 %)	42 (18.4 %)	98 (43.2 %)	69 (30.4 %)	60 (26.4 %)
School helps me develop my own sense of Welshness	107 (46.9 %)	80 (35.1 %)	41 (18 %)	94 (41.4 %)	64 (28.2 %)	69 (30.4 %)

Table 4.3 Longitudinal analysis of living in Wales questions

	Sweep 1 (n = 227)		Sweep 3 (n = 228)	
	Definitely	Definitely Not	Definitely	Definitely Not
When you are an adult, do you think you will live in Wales?	64 (28.2 %)	20 (8.8 %)	31 (13.7 %)	43 (18.9 %)
When you are an adult, do you think you'll live in the same neighbourhood as you do now?	14 (6.2 %)	75 (33.3 %)	12 (5.3 %)	92 (40.4 %)

horizons may expand and suddenly the Welsh countryside and cityscapes they once called home may seem too small to accommodate their hopes and aspirations. Of course, this is merely speculation, and without additional information, it is impossible to know for sure exactly why these young people are less likely to live in Wales as adults. However, perhaps comparing Curriculum Cymreig statements to the responses for the Living in Wales questions for each sweep can suggest a potential relationship between the perceived effects of the Curriculum Cymreig on their appreciation of Wales and their decision to live there as an adult. This analysis is not a causal statement. I am not suggesting that pupils will decide to live in Wales as adults based on their belief that school helped them appreciate living in Wales as a child. However, I am suggesting the results of this comparison can help us to understand pupils' perceptions of, and relationship to, Wales at the time the surveys were completed (Table 4.4).

In both sweeps, over half of the pupils who said they would "Definitely" live in Wales as adults agreed that school helped them appreciate living in Wales. In Sweep 1, 40% of the pupils who would "Definitely not" live in Wales also disagreed that school helped them appreciate living in Wales. In Sweep 3, this percentage increased to 51.2%.

As illustrated above, less than 40% of pupils in Sweep 1 felt that school helps them appreciate living in Wales or to develop their own sense of Welshness. When looking at particular groups within the sample, Year 8 pupils and pupils with higher levels of fluency in Welsh are more likely to agree with these statements. Pupils who self-identified as possessing a Welsh national identity are more likely to agree that schooling helps

Table 4.4 Comparing Curriculum Cymreig and living and feeling at home in Wales

	School helps me appreciate living in Wales					
	Sweep 1 (n=223)			*Sweep 2 (n=222)*		
When you are an adult, do you think you will live in Wales?	*Agree*	*Neither agree nor disagree*	*Disagree*	*Agree*	*Neither agree nor disagree*	*Disagree*
Definitely	36 (57.1%)	18 (28.6%)	9 (14.3%)	18 (58.1%)	11 (35.5%)	2 (6.5%)
Definitely not	5 (25%)	7 (35%)	8 (40%)	10 (24.4%)	10 (24.4%)	21 (51.2%)

them develop their own sense of Welshness. Finally, pupils in the BME ethnicity category were less likely to agree, and more likely to disagree, that school helped them develop their own sense of Welshness, suggesting that schools in Wales underserve ethnic minority pupils in regard to the variables discussed here. These results raise important questions regarding the philosophy, aims, and impact of the Curriculum Cymreig. In isolating two of the aims of the Curriculum Cymreig and situating them as measures to evaluate pupils' beliefs about school and how they construct feelings of affiliation and cultural and national identity, I hoped to provide an insight into the efficacy of the curriculum and its effect on pupils' lives. If the development of national identity, and positive orientations and affiliations with Wales, is an important enough matter to require its own form of curricular intervention, then close attention must be paid to not only its development and implementation but also assessments of its impact set against the aims and goals provided in the guidance document.

STUDY IV: TEACHING WELSHNESS

In 2015, I invited a number of teachers in secondary schools and colleges in Wales to participate in an interview about CE in Wales, and, in particular, how themes of Welshness were addressed in the GCSE, PSE, and Welsh Baccalaureate curricula. As noted above, some of the students I interviewed in 2008 said they felt they learned about Welshness mostly through Welsh lessons, as in Welsh as a second language. A handful of others mentioned history lessons as their source of knowledge about what it means to be Welsh. These responses were expected, because many of the themes and outcomes addressed in the curricula for these classes align well with both discussions of cultural identity and the aims and goals of the Curriculum Cymreig. History and Welsh language lessons naturally lend themselves to the discourse put forward by the Curriculum Cymreig, which promotes traditional representations of Welshness.

However, since the Curriculum Cymreig is one of the flagship policies of Welsh education and one of the main components of what the Welsh Government believes is a system of education distinct from the rest of the UK, I was concerned with how teachers interpret discourses of citizenship and Welshness in the curriculum. While the GCSE curriculum is more accurately understood as a theoretical framework for schooling within a local and global citizenship context, PSE and Welsh Baccalaureate curricula are more aligned to curricula producing lesson plans and traditional forms of instruction. Equally important to the macro-level (school-wide) and micro-level (classroom) interpretations of citizenship and identity is the theoretical grounding of the Curriculum Cymreig. The concepts of citizenship and Welshness in the policy demonstrate how CE in Wales is organised through a broader policy-based perspective. It is a political strategy as much as it is an educational policy. Communitarian approaches to citizenship, highlighting local, communal perspectives and associated living situated within discourses of a distinctively Welsh cultural narrative underscore how citizenship is to be interpreted and portrayed in schools in Wales. I wanted to know how these discourses were mobilised through teachers' curricula and pedagogical practices. I wanted to know how they were prepared to engage in these often complex curricular discussions with their pupils, what materials were provided to them, and, in general, how these themes were received by the pupils and students in their lessons.

After analysing curriculum guidance, speaking with students, and surveying pupils, it was only natural that I speak to teachers about how cultural identity and specifically Welshness are taught in school. Conducting research with teachers is often difficult, not because of the teachers themselves, but because of the nature of schooling. Teachers have long hours. They are at school before the pupils arrive and stay behind long after they're gone. They are cleaning their rooms, planning their lessons, marking assignments, calling parents, attending professional development, attending staff meetings, and more. Their time is precious, and it can be difficult for them to accommodate researchers because of these demands on their time. In addition, schooling has become an environment dominated by "the gaze." ESTYN inspections, head teacher observations, parental and pupil involvement call for accountability from boards of governors and LEAs—all in all, the profile of responsibility has increased while the overall professionalism and autonomy once enjoyed by teachers has been eroded. In this environment, many teachers are sceptical of allowing "outsiders" into their classrooms. In some cases, they can be reticent to discuss what it's like to teach their subject, at their school and with their pupils. However, even with these (and other) concerns, there are teachers who genuinely love what they do, the staff, and pupils they work with every day. They have a genuine concern for what is taught and for whom they are teaching, and I was fortunate enough to interview a number of these teachers actively working in classrooms in Wales.

I invited teachers from the nearly 30 schools involved in the WISERD Education study and secondary teachers and college tutors who attended the Cardiff University Welsh Baccalaureate conference in July 2015. I sent interview schedules to the teachers who were interested in participating and arranged for interviews. Over the course of six months, I spoke with teachers in a variety of schools and colleges across Wales, and present data from 12 of these interviews below. As with the student interviews I conducted above, I had a large amount of qualitative data to transcribe, code, and analyse. From this process, I identified 12 interviews that comprehensively addressed the subject of the research. What was remarkable about these interviews was the coherent narrative that ran through each of the discussions.

I provided a semi-structured interview schedule for the teachers participating in this research. In addition to general demographic data, such as gender, age, years teaching, and their teaching qualifications, I also asked them the following questions:

• What do you think are the aims and goals of the Curriculum Cymreig?
• How do you implement a Curriculum Cymreig in your lessons?

For PSE and Welsh Baccalaureate instructors, I asked them specifically about citizenship and Welshness

• How might you address citizenship or Welshness in one of your lessons?

I also asked the teachers to describe specific classroom experiences, such as "please tell me about a time when you and your pupils discussed Welshness or the Welsh identity" and "please tell me about a time when you discussed citizenship with your pupils." These prompts generated fascinating discussions of how the teachers engaged their students in what could be, at times, difficult conversations. Additionally, I also asked the teachers what they liked and disliked about how cultural identity and citizenship is presented to pupils in schools, as well as how they are trained and supported in teaching their content area. I analysed the teachers' responses using content and thematic analysis. I listened to our discussions repeatedly, and then took notes focusing on recurrent themes and significant passages I felt expressed the teachers' perspective in sophisticated and nuanced ways. After their responses were organised into large thematic categories, I identified more discrete codes and arranged the data into subcategories when possible. As a result, I was able to identify areas of strength and areas for development in the treatment of cultural identity and citizenship from the teachers' perspective. In what follows, I present the data from my interviews with the teachers organised by the themes emerging from their responses. As with the previous studies in this chapter, I discuss the implications of these findings in Chap. 5.

The 12 teachers presented in this research come from all walks of life. Eight of the teachers were female and four of them were male. Collectively, they represented over 82 years of teaching in secondary school, primary school, and college. The teacher with the longest career had taught for 26 years, while the teacher with the shortest had been teaching secondary school for two. Eleven of the teachers held a Post-Graduate Certificate in Education (PGCE), while one—a teacher who taught a GCSE level citizenship class—took an alternative pathway into teaching. The 12 teachers held bachelor degrees in a variety of disciplines including education studies, psychology, geography, history, maths, and early years education. Many of them held graduate degrees, but my purpose for highlighting their qualifications is not to demonstrate their level of education but rather to draw attention to the initial areas of training they received. Nine of the 12 teachers taught exclusively in Wales, while the remaining 3 also had teaching experience in England. All of the teachers were white, with the exception of a female primary teacher of Jamaican heritage. Four of the teachers taught primary school, six taught PSE, Welsh Baccalaureate General Certificate of Secondary Education (GCSE) and citizenship lessons in secondary school, and two taught Welsh Baccalaureate A-Level in college. In regard to geography, the teachers were located in schools in the Cardiff, the Valleys, and Swansea areas.

The Curriculum Cymreig

All of the teachers I interviewed were aware of the Curriculum Cymreig. Nine of the 12 teachers were trained in Wales, and, of those 9, all of them had learned of the Curriculum Cymreig during their studies. The remaining three were introduced to the Curriculum Cymreig by the head teacher at their school the first year they were teaching. While this is unsurprising, the teachers mentioned that references to the Curriculum Cymreig were few and far between. For example, Alys, a bubbly teacher at a primary school in the Valleys, said, "I knew about the Curriculum Cymreig while training as a teacher, and then again during my interview with the head teacher, but it was never brought up again until we were preparing for an ESTYN inspection, and the Curriculum Cymreig was one of the criteria on which we would be judged."

Other teachers I interviewed echoed similar statements saying the policy existed on paper, but not necessarily in the classroom. However, that did not mean the teachers were not concerned with helping the pupils recognise Welshness or experience a sense of belonging at school. For example, Angharad is a PSE teacher at a newly built "super school" in the Valleys. She has a bachelor's degree in geography and earned a PGCE a year after she graduated from university. As a PSE teacher, she said it was often difficult to situate her lessons within a "Welsh ethos," as *Developing the Curriculum Cymreig* suggests.

> I don't really think about it in terms of, "how am I going to teach Welshness to the pupils?" I just think it comes out naturally. We talk about life in Wales, the people in it and the places that make Wales *Wales*, and from that we tend to get a sense of what it is to be Welsh, but I don't think I've ever purposefully thought, "I need to make this lesson more Welsh."

Other teachers shared Angharad's perspective. They were aware of the Curriculum Cymreig and its goals and aims, but they were not provided with meaningful instruction on how to implement a Curriculum Cymreig in their lessons. None of the teachers I interviewed had read *Developing the Curriculum Cymreig*, which partially explains why they struggled with the curriculum. However, many teachers also said they did not receive adequate support from their head teachers in incorporating the Curriculum Cymreig into their lessons. Overall, based on these interviews, secondary teachers are less aware of the Curriculum Cymreig and have less support in working with the curriculum than primary teachers. The majority of primary teachers that I spoke to said they had conversations with colleagues and their senior management teams about the Curriculum Cymreig.

The Goals and Aims of the Curriculum Cymreig

When I asked the teachers about the goals and aims of the Curriculum Cymreig, some of them shrugged their shoulders and said "I don't know." Jane was a thoughtful and patient primary school teacher in her midforties. I observed the final few minutes of her last lesson before the children were sent home. After nearly 17 years teaching primary school, she was a well-seasoned professional who loved her job. In asking her about the Curriculum Cymreig, she said,

> "I understand the aims of the Curriculum Cymreig are to ensure children understand the special things about where they live. They in a place that

is different from any other country in the UK, and that it has a history, a language, a different kind of culture. I think the Curriculum Cymreig is an important part of helping children know where they live and what's good about life there."

While none of the teachers described the aims and goals of the Curriculum Cymreig as it is described in the government guidance, the majority of them understood the initiative was concerned with promoting Welshness and attempting to help pupils associate with being Welsh. However, although the teachers had a general understanding of the curriculum, not all of them felt these were aims worth pursuing. When I asked Welsh Baccalaureate teachers in college if they had heard of the Curriculum Cymreig, they said they had not. Once I told them the aims and goals of the curriculum, Tom, an A-Level Welsh Baccalaureate teacher at a college in the Cardiff area, said:

> We have other concerns that are more pressing. A lot of pupils come to college with very few skills. They scraped by their GCSEs and they're scraping by in their A-Levels. We need to focus on helping them develop skills for university and their careers, not with teaching them how to sing the national anthem or to feel more Welsh. That's a personal choice that's up to them, and they'll make that decision with or without a special, "cultural" curriculum.

Primary and secondary teachers were more sympathetic to their pupils developing a sense of Welshness than Tom, although the primary teachers were the most concerned with considerations of cultural identity in school. As mentioned above in my interviews with head teachers, primary schools tend to provide a better interpretation and implementation of a Curriculum Cymreig that more closely matches the intent of the policy, while secondary schools typically conflate the Curriculum Cymreig with the school's Welsh language policy. This orientation to a more sophisticated understanding of the policy is also reflected in the primary teachers' responses here:

> I think it's important to address culture in school, especially when you have pupils from different backgrounds. Talking about culture helps them feel like they are included.

> When we talk about culture in a lesson, we talk about Wales and being Welsh, but we also talk about other people from different cultural backgrounds in

Wales. I guess what I'm trying to say is, I'm trying to help the children learn about themselves and each other in a way that helps them focus on the good things that bring people together regardless of what their cultural background might be.

When I think about my lessons and the Curriculum Cymreig, I think about making sure the children understand that we live in Wales, and that Wales has its own culture, its own language—our own way of doing things, but that doesn't mean that children from other countries can't learn this, or that they can't add to it. At the same time, I want to encourage my pupils to be open and share their culture with others.

Although teachers felt positively about a curriculum that was culturally relevant and appropriate, they did not feel they were adequately prepared to design such curricula. The majority of the teachers I interviewed felt the Curriculum Cymreig was a curricular policy that had potential, but ultimately was not a high priority in the classroom. These teachers indicated they had not received any professional development regarding the Curriculum Cymreig, and that "overall, we are only asked about it occasionally during our evaluations by our head teachers or if there is an upcoming ESTYN inspection." During one interview, a teacher, who was rather exacerbated, asked, "If this is so important, then why haven't they produced new guidance? Why aren't we talking about this as often as we are about PISA and exam scores?" This statement reflects the considerable amount of pressure many of the teachers feel in preparing pupils to pass their exams. These considerations often mean sacrificing learning experiences that included or promote references to Welshness in order to meet the expectations of the school management, pupils, and parents.

Cultural Identity and Welshness

In regard to knowing about and implementing the Curriculum Cymreig, based on the responses from the teachers I interviewed, primary teachers engage the curriculum more completely than others, and this level of engagement becomes less active with secondary teachers. However, conversations about cultural identity, and, in particular, Welshness, are consistently underdeveloped and rarely considered. Pam, a PSE teacher with a degree in Welsh and ten years of experience in the classroom, described how conversations about culture changed as she stopped teaching Welsh as a second language and began teaching PSE.

The PSE curriculum is busy. I'm supposed to talk about health and safety, general skills, STI's—everything. I know citizenship and identity are supposed to be addressed, but you have to make decisions based on what the pupils want to know, what materials and support you receive and what you've been trained to do. When I taught Welsh, I had a lot of discussions about being Welsh, about what it meant to be Welsh, because those conversations helped the pupils understand the importance of the language. But as a PSE teacher, those things just fade into the background, because I have to focus on things that are more important to students now, like avoiding getting pregnant or an STI.

The notion that discussions of cultural identity and Welshness cannot necessarily be addressed in PSE classes are also reflected in the comments of a young, teacher at a high school in Cardiff. Gemma has been teaching for two years. After completing a bachelor's degree in psychology, she worked in the private sector for a while until taking an alternative pathway to teaching. Currently, she teaches A-Level psychology in the school's Sixth Form, as well as a GCSE level citizenship class. When I asked her to tell me about the citizenship course, she said

We typically discuss human rights, how to behave in society, what rights do pupils have, consumers, etc. We talk a lot about community action and active citizenship, democracy and issues in the workplace, but in terms of cultural identity or being Welsh, we don't really talk about those things as much.

Gemma went on to say that the class engages in "debates" over contemporary issues and the ideas of human rights, and that the pupils enjoy these opportunities to argue and discuss these issues, but when I asked her why they did not discuss concepts of cultural identity or Welshness, she said:

I think we might just assume we know what Welshness is, and so we don't really think about addressing it specifically. In regard to cultural identity overall, the curriculum is really more geared towards understanding rights, behaviour and being an active citizen. I believe cultural identity plays into that, but with the way the curriculum is put together, those conversations, if they happen, tend to be unplanned.

Overall, the PSE and Welsh Baccalaureate teachers noted that it is difficult to discuss "culture." They believe discussions of cultural identity are important and have an interest in having these discussions with their pupils and students, but they have difficulty addressing the issue when the curricula for these courses focus on specific outcomes for pupils that do not specifically address cultural identity. More important, however, is they often mentioned they did not have the training necessary to discuss cultural identity or Welshness, or the materials that could provide them with meaningful conversations with pupils about culture and its relationship to citizenship. The following excerpt from the teachers' interviews illustrates their concerns:

> I was trained in maths. I taught math for several years, but when I returned to teaching the only position I could get was teaching PSE lessons. I'm not trained for PSE. Everything I did to get ready to teach PSE I did on my own. I was provided materials left by the previous teachers, but I made the lesson plans and organised the curriculum. When it comes to teaching Welshness, or talking about culture, or teaching about citizenship for that matter, I don't have the same level of expertise that I do in maths.

Since there is no PSE qualification in Wales, all teachers who teach PSE are certified to teach in a different discipline. All of the PSE teachers I interviewed discussed the difficulties of creating what many referred to as a "meaningful learning experience" for pupils with the guidance and materials provided to them by previous teachers or current school leadership, without specific training in teaching concepts of citizenship and culture. At a college level, instructors made important distinctions between what they thought was the intention of the Welsh Baccalaureate qualification and discussions of cultural identity and citizenship:

> The Welsh Bacc is really about skills. Citizenship, global citizenship, those are presented to students because they're an important part of the students' perspective on the world, but the primary focus is preparing them for university and a career.

Both primary and secondary teachers communicated a level of frustration with PSE curricula and the Curriculum Cymreig. They felt these initiatives were promoted as addressing a broad variety of topics and concerns, but, in reality, the implementation and focus on certain issues made it difficult to meaningfully engage pupils in discussion of citizenship and culture. The following is a quote from Meg, a very to-the-point primary school teacher. She has 26 years of experience and concisely summarised these concerns below. Her eyes lit up brightly as she planted the index finger of one hand into her palm as she made her point:

I think things like PSE and the Curriculum Cymreig, they have good intentions, but they don't really hit the mark. If you really want to learn about
cultural identity and Welshness, you have to ask questions like "what is culture, what is Welshness, why is it important?" and we don't do that. The
curriculums don't encourage that and we aren't trained to do it.

Pupils and Citizenship

Overall, these PSE teachers felt they were insufficiently trained for the
lessons they taught. Additionally, all the teachers and instructors I interviewed felt the PSE and Welsh Baccalaureate curricula, and the Curriculum
Cymreig, provided insufficient guidance to meaningfully address the issues
of cultural identity and Welshness. Moreover, they suggested the priori-
ties of certain subjects addressed in PSE and Welsh Baccalaureate lessons
interfered with discussions of citizenship and cultural identity. In other
words, if curriculum is a body of knowledge that educators feel is worth
knowing, "skills" and preparation for university and careers have taken
precedence over citizenship and understanding cultural identity.

Summary

From analysing the discourse of *Developing the Curriculum Cymreig*, surveying pupils, and interviewing students and teachers, I believe the project
for teaching pupils about cultural identity, and, in particular, Welshness, is
beset by a multitude of problems. These issues begin with an unsatisfactory
approach to understanding culture and identity in the guidance provided
to teachers by the Welsh Government. The language of *Developing the
Curriculum Cymreig* presents a multicultural Welshness with a plurality of
definitions and representations, but the examples of best practice included
in the guidance, and the theoretical framing of Welshness that undergird
them, fail to authentically engage concepts of a plural Welshness and primarily convey historically acceptable, ethnocentric representations of Welsh
life and culture. This emerges from a brand of Welshness grounded in historical artefacts and cultural touchstones—a traditionalist perspective of
Welshness that fails to provide teachers and pupils with meaningful opportunities to philosophically engage with Welshness in respect to the historical realities of living in Wales set against their contemporary experiences
and circumstances. In addition to an unsophisticated conceptualisation
of culture and cultural identity, the guidance supporting the Curriculum

Cymreig fails to prepare teachers for incorporating and accommodating meaningful references and connections for pupils to Wales.

In my interviews with students in West Wales, the majority of the young people I spoke to struggled to articulate their feelings about culture and identity. Many of them claimed they never had conversations about culture and Welshness, and as a result they struggled to find language sufficient to describe their understanding and orientation to a Welsh cultural identity. Through their struggles, they often remarked on what they felt was distinctive about Wales, such as the language, and they also mentioned how being Welsh made them feel distinctive. This language matches much of the rhetoric included in *Developing the Curriculum Cymreig*, but the similarities seem to end there. While the guidance for teachers encourages them to create learning experiences emphasising historical and cultural aspects of Welsh culture, such as visiting castles and listening to bards, the young people spoke about Welshness in terms of their social relationships with family and friends, and an overarching sense of community they experience at school and in the areas they call home.

Unsurprisingly, teachers felt overwhelmed by the task of incorporating themes of Welshness into their lessons when (a) their lessons might not always be related to discussions or representations of Wales and (b) they lacked specific guidance from their school and the Welsh Government in designing curricula that meaningfully accommodate themes of Welshness. To further complicate this experience, policy approaches to understanding culture lack a robust theoretical treatment and do not translate well into a pedagogical approach that dialectically deconstructs orientations to culture, identity, and their meaning in our social and culture milieu. Moreover, they felt the pressure from parents and school management for preparing pupils for exams and the priority placed on PISA results took precedence over helping young people to better conceptualise and engage in discussions about culture and identity.

These problems are reflected in the data collected from the pupils' survey results. Clearly, the majority of pupils surveyed did not feel schooling helped them appreciate living in Wales or in developing their own sense of Welshness. Additionally, the number of pupils who feel Wales is their "real home" and would choose to live in Wales when they are adults are important indicators of their association with Wales and Welshness. While a small majority of pupils agreed with these statements, this number fell to a minority as they progressed through schooling. If the Curriculum Cymreig truly had the impact on pupils' education that is stated in the curricular guidance provided by the Welsh Government, then one would expect much different results. In the next chapter, I discuss the findings of these studies and discuss how an enlarged perspective on identity, coupled with a critical pedagogy, might provide teachers and pupils with a more robust approach to teaching and learning about cultural identity that promotes intellectual curiosity, philosophical reasoning, and a grounded dialectical practice encouraging teachers and pupils alike to become critical consumers of culture and curriculum.

REFERENCES

Brubaker, R., & Cooper, F. (2000). Beyond identity. *Theory and Society, 29*, 1–47.
Fairclough, N. (2001). *Language and power* (2nd ed.). New York: Longman.

CHAPTER 5

Reconceptualising the Curriculum Cymreig

Abstract Referring to the work of Brubaker and Cooper (*Theory and Society* 29: 1–47, 2000), Smith emphasises the importance of "moving beyond" current representations of Welshness and adopting more comprehensive approaches to thinking about citizenship and cultural identity. Part of this philosophical approach includes the acknowledgement of the technical rationale-dominated CE curricula and a recommendation to incorporate emancipatory forms of pedagogy that promote critical and political literacy, with the intention that as young people and their teachers engage in a critical pedagogy of identity, they can challenge reified representations of Welshness (and other cultural identities), deconstruct the ways in which these identities are comprised and promoted, and construct new and inclusive approaches to theorising representations of self and others.

Keywords Welshness • Cultural identity • Citizenship • Citizenship Education • Critical Pedagogy

BEYOND WELSHNESS

Identity—a simple word for a complex concept. Identity has withstood the scrutiny of scholars for years, with a vast array of theories, definitions, and approaches that continue to be debated. In order to avoid a lengthy and potentially less useful treatise on the various approaches to identity, I would like to focus on Brubaker and Cooper's attempts to move "beyond" identity, or at least the inadequate use of the word "identity"

81
K. Smith, *Curriculum, Culture and Citizenship Education in Wales*,
DOI 10.1057/978-1-137-54443-8_5

in attempting to describe the ways in which we come to know our self/ selves and present that self/those selves to others. In short, Brubaker and Cooper (2000) argue that constructivists' views on identity undermine attempts to analyse the concept. They believe there is an identity crisis in the analysis of identity(ies) in the social sciences due to the ways in which the complexity of the term is "torn between 'hard' and 'soft' meanings, essentialist connotations and constructivist qualifiers" (p. 2). Brubaker and Cooper (2000) refer to Bourdieu in asserting that identity is a category both of practice and of analysis. A category of practice refers to the daily social interaction and experience constructed and acted out by ordinary people in their daily lives.

In the everyday sense, identity is used to help individuals to make sense of their social setting and activity within it. In addition, as is the case with the representations of Welshness in *Developing the Curriculum Cymreig*, identity is used for political purposes to "persuade people to understand themselves, their interests, and their predicaments in a certain way, to persuade certain people that they are (for certain purposes) 'identical' with one another and at the same time different from others" (Brubaker and Cooper 2000, p. 5). The use of identity as a category of practice does not preclude it from also operating as a category of analysis, or the ways in which categories of identity are constructed and used in attempts to describe their psychological and sociological roles. These categories are constructed, promoted, and mobilised by scholars, academics, and other "intellectuals" for social and political reasons, much like categories of practice. In addition, they are often used much in the same way as categories of practice, meaning they are used in ways that reify the categories, giving them a sense of concreteness and essentialist reality rather than socially constructed organisational types.

In addition to these category types, Brubaker and Cooper also suggest a multidimensional ambiguity of identity as it is discussed in contemporary research and theory, which undermines the concept of identity and paralyses new ways of conceiving and reacting to identity. For example, "strong" and "weak" conceptions of identity are two key ways in which the identity is semantically phrased. This phrasing can complicate and nullify (to a degree) approaches to understanding identity. Strong approaches "preserve the common-sense meaning of the term," while weak approaches "break consciously with the everyday meaning of the term" (Brubaker and Cooper 2000, p. 10). In negotiating these (and other) approaches to identity, Brubaker and Cooper suggest the following lenses through which one might view identity. These multiple lenses provide a more complex and articulated framework for thinking about how we construct and engage with identity.

- Identification and categorisation
- Self-understanding and social location
- Commonality, connectedness, groupness

As I mentioned before, the theoretical framework for identity and culture that serves as the rationale for Curriculum Cymreig is underdeveloped and too narrow in focus. Andrews and Lewis (2000) suggest the Curriculum Cymreig is too closely associated with concepts of "cultural citizenship," or a way of thinking about citizenship that is established upon traditional practices or intergenerational transmission of association through bloodlines or familial relationships. This is a form of citizenship that emerges from nationalistic conceptions of culture and identity, and contrasts strongly with other models of citizenship, such as active and global citizenship, both of which make more concessions for a plural, multicultural citizenship and a larger appeal for rights and privileges of people. At the heart of a cultural citizenship is a form of "authentic" or "essential" identity, a standard from which other claims to identity can be measured. This discourse of authenticity is a strong practical category of identity that is used as a form of differentiation and demarcation. In the rhetoric of the Curriculum Cymreig, the discourse of essentialism and authenticity is softened as it is mobilised through the term "distinctive." This is possible through technical approaches to discussing citizenship and identity that I describe below, but, more important, these categories of practice and analysis, of strong and weak phrasings of identity, help to explain the representations of Welshness put forward in the Curriculum Cymreig and also the ways pupils and teachers make meaning of cultural identity in their everyday life.

For example, the first lens mentioned by Brubaker and Cooper, *Identification and categorization*, is regarded as processes that avoid the "reifying connotations of 'identity'" (Brubaker and Cooper 2000, p. 14). The *Developing the Curriculum Cymreig* document lacks in a robust and engaging theoretical and philosophical treatment of Welshness, or even identification. Similarly, the official guidance for PSE and ESDGC provided to schools and teachers suffer from the same condition. However, what is included in the guidance for the Curriculum Cymreig is a discussion of

Welshness that promotes an assumptive, commonsensical view of cultural identity that circumvents scrutiny and attempts to promote Welshness as something which exists and is waiting for pupils to experience. This rhetoric reflects what Brubaker and Cooper regard as "reifying connotations of identity," in that the distinctiveness and value of Welshness is regarded as real, concrete, and so obviously apparent that it does not require methods for construction and deconstruction, but rather simple exploration and discovery, as is demonstrated through the case studies included in the guidance.

However, in my discussions with young people and teachers, these discussions did not presuppose they all had similar understandings and orientations to Welshness. Identification and categorisation are active terms that "invite us to specify the agents that do the identifying" (Brubaker and Cooper 2000, p. 14). My discussions of identity and Welshness enabled students and teachers to identify actors involved in the representation and construction of Welshness. This situational and contextual process is central to our everyday experience, while identity as a concept is not. Overall, Welshness, as an identity communicated through school curricula, is presented to teachers and young people as a finished product and does not recognise the process of identification and categorisation.

Self-understanding and social location are "dispositional terms" that designate "one's sense of who one is, of one's social location, and of how (given the first two) one is prepared to act" (Brubaker and Cooper 2000, p. 17). Similar to identification and categorisation, this lens resists the reifying value of identity and also acknowledges the cognitive awareness of the individual in navigating self, others, and the social landscape in which these actors engage in the meaning-making processes of their everyday lives. Discursive formations, or "patterns of regularity in terms of order, correlation, position and function" (Macey 2001, p. 101), representing Welshness often circumvent scrutiny and critique, establishing such representations as commonsensical and grounded in objectivity. However, self-understanding acknowledges the subjective nature of identification and challenges weak understandings of identity, allowing for opportunity to elaborate on the social, cultural, political, and other circumstances that contribute to one's sense of self.

In my discussions with young people and teachers, their attempts to articulate a sense of Welshness, or more appropriately their own sense of Welshness, often avoided this concept of self-understanding and social location. Instead, they first relied on objective, easily definable representations of Welshness that had been readily available through a constant exposure to discursive formations of Welshness. Rugby, cawl, and even the Welsh language became relatively empty signifiers that, instead of focusing on a personalised experience or sense of Welshness, pointed to previously existing conceptual blocs of Welshness. However, as I continued to explore their responses through probing questions, they were better able to unpack a more subjective approach to communicating their understanding of cultural identity. Through a dialectical process of questioning, answering, and questioning again, the participants began to situate their discussion of Welshness within the subjective rhetoric of their experience, and this process of self-understanding and location provided them with a much more rich and rewarding process for thinking about cultural identity.

Commonality, connectedness, groupness are emotionally laden senses of "belonging to a distinctive, bounded group, involving both a felt solidarity or oneness with fellow group members and a felt difference from or even antipathy to specific outsiders" (Brubaker and Cooper 2000, p. 19). The rhetoric of the Curriculum Cymreig insists on establishing the distinctiveness of Welshness, and while Welshness, like all cultural identities, has distinctive elements to it that differentiate it from other lived experiences, at times the rhetoric of the guidance supporting the policy seems more concerned with establishing difference than recognising commonality. The terms used in this lens may seem to promote a unifying "oneness" or common affiliation, but that is not the intention. Brubaker and Cooper underscore this point in writing that this set of terms is intended to "develop an analytical idiom sensitive to the multiple forms and degrees of commonality and connectedness, and to the widely varying ways in which actors (and the cultural idioms, public narratives and prevailing discourses on which they draw) attribute meaning and significance to them" (Brubaker and Cooper 2000).

A discourse that is open to concepts of commonality and connectedness is one of the primary features I noticed in students' responses describing Welshness. Initially, some pupils mobilised existing discursive formations in describing Welshness much in the same way as the Curriculum Cymreig guidance, emphasising distinction and difference rather than exploring, or even accommodating, commonalities and connectedness. For example, a popular response to what does it mean to be Welsh was "to not be English." This was a simple, commonsensical assertion that anything English could not be Welsh, but it hardly reflects the reality of commonality and connectedness experienced by many people in the

UK. As our conversations continued, however, more and more concepts of connectedness and groupness could be found in the students' responses. One important distinction of these terms is that they still allow for difference, for distinction, while also accommodating association and commonality. Young people who may feel particularly Welsh can still experience a connection to a person who feels particularly English, and this non-binary process of identification better reflects the realities of our social, cultural, and political relationships.

In attempting to move "beyond identity," Brubaker and Cooper have provided a model from which a more nuanced and articulated approach to teaching and learning Welshness can be developed. Rather than relying on a technical rationale in conceptualising citizenship that promotes objective knowledge and assumptive understandings of culture formalised through promoting traditional practices that mask social and political motivations, a rephrasing of identity and how we come to terms with the concept can allow for disestablishing the reification of assumed representations of Welshness (and other cultural identities). This disestablishment of objectivity promoted through discursive formations of Welshness can lead teachers and young people to be critical connoisseurs of curriculum and develop a broader sense of critical literacy overall, which, in turn, can possibly lead to more sophisticated understandings of one's self and others, a greater engagement in forms of citizenship and the circumstances necessary to improve our methods of associated living.

CURRICULARISING WELSHNESS

In the first sweep of surveying Year 8 and Year 10 pupils, the data revealed that less than 40% believe school helped them appreciate living in Wales or develop their own sense of Welshness. Additionally, BME pupils were more likely to disagree than white pupils that school helped them in this regard. Finally, in Year 10, there was a significant drop in the number of pupils who agreed to these statements compared to pupils in Year 8. In short, according to pupils' responses, the Curriculum Cymreig is failing in its objectives and aims, and, in fact, as pupils move from primary to secondary school and to their later years of compulsory education, it is having little to no effect.

My analysis of school documents and interview data reveals that head teachers and staff of both primary and secondary schools interpret the Curriculum Cymreig policy too narrowly, focusing on either red dragons and daffodils or Welsh language use rather than larger discussions of how pupils can think about culture and understand its role in their lives. The reasons for this failure to accommodate a more philosophical approach to culture and curriculum are manifold. For example, the guidance for teachers fails to address theoretical discussions of culture and how teachers can address such concerns in their classrooms. Instead, the guidance focuses primarily on providing opportunities for pupils to experience authentically "Welsh" activities and traditions (Smith 2010). The interview data demonstrate schools' concern with pupils' academic achievement based on exam results and school inspections, and that this emphasis can dominate educational practice, limiting opportunities to discuss concerns that are not specifically assessed or measured. Finally, CE and discussions of the cultural dimensions of citizenship in Wales are relegated to PSE and ESDGC classes, which often become "catch all" courses that fail to accommodate in-depth and robust discussions of the content at hand.

Overall, primary schools in my research demonstrated a greater concern in performing a Curriculum Cymreig and enacting it as much more of a school-wide approach that promoted a Welsh ethos and not just a language policy. In many cases, the Curriculum Cymreig was perceived as an element of schooling through which pupils could become aware of their cultural and communal associations in addition to their learning activities. In addition, the head teachers of primary schools were also less likely to frame the enactment of a Curriculum Cymreig solely within the language of ESTYN (the education and training inspectorate for Wales) inspections and policy, while the head teachers of the secondary schools regularly referenced ESTYN inspections and reports.

The broader, more accessible interpretation of the Curriculum Cymreig in primary schools and its outward expression in the classrooms and corridors could help explain why Year 8 pupils are more likely to feel that school positively impacts their appreciation of Wales and sense of Welshness. In secondary schools, the interpretation of the Curriculum Cymreig is situated almost entirely within the context of Welsh language use and meeting the criteria of ESTYN inspections. This means–end approach to curriculum implementation fails to engage pupils and teachers alike. As a result, particularly in secondary schools, the emphasis on academic outcomes and qualifications overshadow concerns for promoting a Welsh ethos. The current mandate for teachers to squeeze a "Welsh dimension" into their regular lesson plans is an ineffective method to help pupils explore their associations and perception or Wales, or to think about how they construct their own sense of cultural identity. After two years of secondary school, Year 10 pupils may not believe that school positively affects their appreciation of Wales and sense of Welshness because the degree to which schools address these issues is greatly compromised.

As evidenced through interview data and school documents, school Welsh language policies dominate conversations of curriculum and culture in Wales. Literacy in Cymraeg is a distinctive feature of Welsh education and a socially, culturally, and politically important policy concern. However, the primacy of literacy in Welsh dominates other Welsh culture concerns and shapes the way in which head teachers and their staff understand and enact curriculum. Participants who were more fluent in Welsh agreed that school helped them appreciate living in Wales and develop their own sense of Welshness far more than pupils who were less fluent. Apart from the important role language plays in cultural identity, concerns over "Cymraeg" (Welsh language) far outweigh curricular conversations of "Cymreig" (Welsh culture). Pupils' learning experiences in schools in Wales are intersected by Welsh language policy, and in regard to the cultural dimension of CE, these concerns dominate discussions of what it is to be Welsh and what that might mean in regard to pupils' concerns of their cultural and national identity, and conceptions of what it means to be a citizen in Wales.

Finally, in regard to Welshness and ethnicity, apart from the challenges ethnic minority pupils face in schools in Wales, there simply are not enough discussions regarding how to create a more inclusive and accessible Welshness for these pupils. Of the 838 pupils participating in Sweep 1, 96 were self-identified as non-White. The pupils attend schools dominated by Whiteness and constructions of Welshness emerging from within and without that context. In the interviews with head teachers, only two mentioned how measures were taken to help non-White pupils and pupils born outside of Wales to engage in Welshness at their schools. Unsurprisingly, these schools possess large numbers of ethnic minority pupils. However, non-White pupils and pupils born outside of Wales can be found in nearly all the participants. The lack of discussion of ethnic minorities and Welshness corresponds to the absence of such concerns from the guidance outlining the Curriculum Cymreig. In this document, general rhetoric is employed in discussing a plural and multicultural Wales, but apart from an example in Religious Education lessons, none of the case studies presented provided serious guidance for teachers on how to transcend constructions of a white Welsh–Welshness into a more accurate and relevant multicultural understanding of the complexities of Wales' history and culture (Smith 2010). If national guidance does not contain viable strategies for multicultural citizenship that can be implemented in schools, the likelihood of such activities being taken in schools in Wales is greatly reduced.

LOCATING WELSHNESS

The statements from the second sweep of the study included in Chap. 4 referred pupils' associations with Welshness and their sense of belonging and home in Wales. Unsurprisingly, pupils who self-identified as Welsh were more likely to agree that they would live in Wales as opposed to other locations and that Wales is their real home. They were also less likely to agree that they live in Wales but do not particularly feel Welsh. What this question tells us is that approximately 30% of the pupils feel a strong connection to Wales—a strong enough connection that they prefer Wales to any other part of the world. The motivation to stay in Wales can be connected to a number of reasons apart from a sense of belonging or wanting to live in Wales. Family, friends, economy, and lifestyle choices all play a part in our decisions to settle down, and while the Curriculum Cymreig addresses the importance of these factors in the lives of young people, its representation of Wales and Welshness may not engage pupils in ways that promote a sense of belonging and affiliation. In a study I recently published in the *Journal of Environmental Education Research* (Smith 2015), I demonstrated how pupils' perceptions of the areas in which they live differ vastly from the guidance provided for teachers in enacting a Curriculum Cymreig in their classrooms. Where the guidance emphasised cultural and historical touchstones as the means through which pupils can come to know and "appreciate" the areas of Wales in which they live, through the qualitative data provided by pupils it seems they construct the place identities of their local areas through the quality and nature of their relational and experiential values of their relationships and environments. In other words, the young people surveyed tend to describe the areas in which they live through descriptions of the personalities and characteristics of the people who live there and the value of the relationships the young people have with them. Additionally, when the pupils did address the geography of Wales and the ambient qualities of the physical reality of the places where they live, they did so in emotive terms, often describing how their areas made them "feel."

These descriptions mark a considerable departure from the language of the Curriculum Cymreig guidance and suggest a disconnect between curricular representations and pupils' orientations to place. The data included above suggest that the Curriculum Cymreig policy does not necessarily positively impact pupils' affiliations with Wales or increase their appreciation of the "distinctiveness of living in Wales" (Welsh Government 2003).

When the findings of the Home statements from Sweep 2 are compared to the Curriculum Cymreig statements of Sweep 1, the relationship between the potential of the Curriculum Cymreig in promoting a sense of belonging in pupils seems even less convincing. Crosstab comparisons between pupils who agree with the Curriculum Cymreig and Home statements suggest no significant positive relationships between young people's perceptions of the impact of schooling on their affiliation with Wales and Welshness, and their motivations to live in Wales as adults or their sense of home. The reasons for this are many, and unfortunately cannot be determined by the data collected. Whether the philosophical framework of the Curriculum Cymreig is insufficient for pupils to meaningfully engage in understanding and constructing a coherent and personalised orientation to Welshness or whether the actual interpretation and implementation of the Curriculum Cymreig in schools is lacking is difficult to say. However, based on the evidence I have collected and my years researching the Curriculum Cymreig, I suspect it is a combination of these factors and more. Further research is required to pick apart the complexities of curricular policies and treatments intended to promote and engender positive orientations to cultural and national identity.

In Chap. 4, the Curriculum Cymreig statements were repeated to pupils in Sweep 3, allowing the data to take on a longitudinal dimension. Unsurprisingly, similar to the results of Sweep 1, the pupils were less likely to agree that the Curriculum Cymreig statements helped them appreciate living in Wales or develop their own sense of Welshness. In fact, as stated above, not only were less pupils likely to agree, but the percentage of pupils who were initially ambivalent in Sweep 1 also decreased as the percentage of pupils who disagreed increased. These findings reinforce the possibility that the interpretation and implementation of the Curriculum Cymreig in secondary schools is not as effective as approaches to the policy in primary schools.

In addition to the Curriculum Cymreig statements, the Living in Wales questions from Sweep 1 were also repeated. As before, the pupils were less likely to agree they would live in Wales as adults. Similar to the Home statements, the reasons for this change are unclear and require further research using qualitative research methods.

Overall, across the three sweeps of data collection, pupils' responses have shifted negatively, demonstrating that as they progress through school, they feel school has less of an impact on their appreciation of living in Wales and their ability to develop a sense of Welshness. Furthermore, as they progress through school they are less likely to say they feel Wales is their "real home" or that they feel Welsh. Finally, the percentage of children in school who say they want to live in Wales as adults also decreases. These findings are counterintuitive when considering that these children have attended schools where a compulsory curricular initiative designed to engender feelings of appreciation, belonging, and strong ties to cultural identity is purportedly enmeshed into the ethos of their schools. Based on these data, if the Welsh Government truly wants to achieve the aims and goals outlined in *Developing the Curriculum Cymreig*, then the guidance for teachers must be reconceptualised, offering an attempt to "move beyond" nationalistic and traditional conceptions of identity and to include ways in which head teachers can incorporate the policy into their school's ethos, and discussions of how cultural identity and citizenship are understood in schools must include pedagogical engagements founded on philosophical inquiry and critical methods of investigation and instruction.

CRITICAL APPROACHES TO CITIZENSHIP AND IDENTITY

In the remainder of this chapter, I hope to demonstrate how the incorporation of a critical perspective in Welsh curricula and pedagogy can assist in developing a type of political literacy that enables pupils and teachers to recognise discursive practices that manufacture consent through the mobilisation of ideological assumptions and "commonsensical" knowledge in educational discourse, particularly as it relates to understanding representations of Welshness in citizenship curricula in Wales. One central concept that rests at the centre of this chapter is that of political literacy. The purpose of developing political literacy is to recognise ideological assumptions that present fixed, limited realities for individuals in society, and to reveal the limited nature of this reality as something that is, in all actuality, dynamic and subject to change through the conscious application of an individual's praxis (Freire 2006). In educational terms, political literacy involves the application of a critical perspective and reasoning that enables in individuals the ability to see the varied forces that affect contemporary education.

The established discourses of Welshness in citizenship curricula in Wales, and the practices associated with those discourses, act as considerable organisational elements of the Welsh cultural identity that supplant philosophical considerations among teachers and students. Instead of being able to ruminate and dialectically discuss the nature, purpose, and value of culture, and, in particular, Welshness, discursive formations comprising supposedly legitimised claims are quietly and unthinkingly consumed. Much of this occurs in classrooms in schools, when potential debates and deconstructions of culture and its role in developing citizenship are diverted to banal platitudes of Welshness set within established, rigid narratives of cultural citizenship and nationalism.

Such uncritical and ineffectual engagements with culture and citizenship reveal the soporific effect the Curriculum Cymreig has on pupils' orientations to Wales and Welshness. As evidenced in the previous chapter, pupils overwhelmingly disagree schooling has a positive impact on their appreciation of life in Wales or their capacity to develop their own sense of Welshness, which can be interpreted as a pseudonym for a sense of citizenship that reflects upon life and responsibility from Wales, in Wales and beyond. In Chap. 4, teachers echoed the difficulties of meaningfully implementing a curriculum that contains no viable philosophical treatment of citizenship or culture, and that merely presents hollow rhetoric which fails to engage the imagination or occupy the pedagogical possibilities inherent in their practice.

At first glance, the goals of the Curriculum Cymreig seem admirable, as if they can provide teachers with the means to frame more developed discussions of citizenship in PSE and Welsh Baccalaureate lessons. However, the aims are discussed in a way that assumes that a sense of Welshness already exists. In addition, the text relies upon established discourses and stereotypes in producing representative experiences of Welshness for pupils at the expense of alternative and marginalised conceptualisations of what it might mean to be Welsh in Wales. These traditional discourses fail to engage contemporary elements of pupils' identity and citizenship. What about gay Wales? Where is Black Wales? When was/is a woman's Wales? The Curriculum Cymreig is intended to allow pupils an opportunity to directly experience Wales and Welshness. It is the curricular backbone for instructional considerations of identity and citizenship in Wales, and it intends for each pupil to identify a personal sense of Welshness from her/his own experience. However, in addition to the traditional caricatures of Welshness promoted in the curricular guidance, the overall organisation of the policy continues to privilege a white, heterosexual male discourse of Welshness that fails to establish meaningful excavations of Welshness that speak to the realities of pupils living in Wales.

CRITICAL PEDAGOGY AND THE CURRICULUM CYMREIG

My own orientation to education is heavily influenced by the work of Paulo Freire, Henry Giroux, and others whose work is often associated with that of critical pedagogy. Although many of these scholars are identified as possessing varied, often disparate, philosophical/ideological orientations to education, these differences highlight the interdisciplinary nature of critical pedagogy and its ability to be used as a helpful tool in transforming school. As schools serve as powerful institutions that produce and reproduce knowledge and culture in society (Apple 2004), those working in the tradition of critical pedagogy see schools as prime locations for the transformation of societal structures and their attendant discursive practices placing limitations on pupils and obfuscating the mechanisms of oppression. This is a key characteristic of critical pedagogy; the efforts associated with this approach to education are not focused in attacking and eliminating socially unjust circumstances from society, but, rather, in transforming society as a whole. The goal is not an excision of unjust practices and world views but the creation of a reality in which these practices and perspectives cannot exist. Advocates of critical pedagogy argue, among other positions, that people should "understand the nature of oppression in modern society" and understand how their "ascribed characteristics (e.g., race, class, gender) and their culture impact on that oppression" (Sleeter and Grant 2003, p. 190). This understanding of multiple forms of oppression, and the varied components of social life which intersect it, is dependent upon the development of political literacy. Freire (1985) describes the importance of political literacy in terms of understanding the world as a transformable reality.

> A political illiterate—regardless of whether she or he knows how to read and write—is one who… has a naive outlook on social reality, which for this one is a given, that is, social reality is a fait accompli rather than something that's still in the making. (p. 103)

In Wales, an official school curriculum is manifested in the creation of outcomes disseminated to schools from a bureaucratic political body that governs educational policies and its varied ancillary organisations. In his work, Freire regularly used the word "oppression." Often, this word is understood on a grand scale because it is associated with large-scale violence, dehumanisation, and control. However, it can also occur in small, incremental steps. It is these smaller incursions of the liberty of teachers and students that I refer to when I discuss oppression in school. Oppression in education is subtle and varied. For example, pupils who do not see themselves represented within a school's curriculum are often objectified and alienated by it. This is a form of oppression that often goes unnoticed by the majority because they are blinded by their privilege and the norm to which the curriculum is oriented. Irrespective of the rhetoric contained in *Developing the Curriculum Cymreig*, ethnocentricity and nationalistic assumptions continue to undermine the efficacy of the policy.

Those working in the field of critical pedagogy are, among other concerns, interested in ways in which social institutions project an objectifying world view in society. In Wales, the Curriculum Cymreig seems to have been developed in response to postcolonial discourses produced through its hegemonic relationship over the centuries with England. In terms of how the text situates Welshness as a distinctive identity in response to English hegemony, it seems supremely interested in creating a distinctive identity to that of England and the other home countries, as well as a politically viable nation. The process of nation-building and a desire for people to self-identify as Welsh has trumped philosophical considerations of what is cultural identity, why it is important, and what role it plays in society. In each of my studies presented in this book, I was persistently reminded of the need for teachers and pupils to philosophically and critically reflect upon representations of Welshness in the curriculum—to develop a critical and political literacy that would enlarge their capacity to engage with the content of the curriculum and not passively receive it.

Such a process is described by Freire as conscientisation, or the ability to "perceive social, political, and economic contradictions, and to take action against the oppressive elements of reality" (Freire 1985, p. 67). Freire asserts the goal of conscientisation is "to provoke recognition of the world, not as a 'given' world, but as a world dynamically 'in the making'" (Ibid.), and this speaks directly to empowerment. Teachers and pupils can also be empowered through incorporating a critical perspective in education, especially in regard to how they engage in discussions of self-identification and associations with cultural identity. I firmly believe opportunities must be provided in schools where pupils can develop a conscious awareness of the variable factors that affect their living and learning in society, and to achieve a level of political literacy that gives them the ability to act upon this awareness in real and meaningful ways. In discussing conscientisation and its importance in empowering individuals to take part in the identi-fication of limited situations, Freire states conscientisation is more than a simple prise de conscience. While it implies overcoming "false conscious-ness," overcoming, that is, a semiintransitive or naive transitive state of consciousness, it implies further the critical insertion of the conscientised person into a demythologised reality (Freire 1985, p. 85).

The critical insertion of the conscientised person is a step towards the empowering of individuals to interact with and transform a reality they once regarded as limited situations. These discourses assist in the mytholo-gising of the education process as a fixed situation, a limited reality that is static and resistant to change. In short, both teachers and their pupils are faced with obstacles which limit their perception of reality. Teachers, pupils, and parents—community members critically engaged in challeng-ing, questioning, and investigating the educational reality presented to them—can give voice to alternative discourses in society that transcend the supposed boundaries of what is and is not possible in education today. Through this conscious effort in analysing and critiquing the discursive practices maintained within the institution of education, they can deter-mine the discourse of their own representation and provide multiple path-ways leading to their orientation to self, community, and nation.

New Approaches to Citizenship and Cultural Identity

As mentioned previously, curriculum and ideology are intricately entwined (Apple 2004). The onto-epistemological considerations of curricular development, along with political ideologies and discourses of power, and have been scrutinised and critiqued by scholars concerned with schooling existing as a critical practice that informs and promotes human eman-cipation (Aronowitz and Giroux 1993 ; Gillborn 2006; Giroux 1981, 2010a). While pupils and teachers can gain a more robust understanding of the plurality of Wales and greater association with Welshness through the development of their critical literacy (Apple 2008; Bates 2006; Freire 1985, 2000; Giroux 2010b, 2011, 2012), I also want to address how approaches to citizenship can either undermine or contribute to a criti-cally empowered perspective on citizenship and culture. Specifically, I turn to Giroux's discussion of critical theory and three modes of rationality regularly present in models of CE curricula—the Technical, Hermeneutic, and Emancipatory (Giroux 1980). Giroux describes the connection between models of citizenship transmission in CE curricula and technical rationale, stating that knowledge is "fixed and unchanging in the sense that its form, structure, and underlying normative assumptions appear to be universalized beyond the realm of historical contingency or critical analysis" (p. 337). In short, the transmission of knowledge of citizenship is natural, objective, and not necessarily subject to critique or review. Furthermore, it privileges a less complicated social landscape that downplays conflict and "neither recognizes or responds to social and structural dysfunctions" (p. 338).

Unlike models of citizenship transmission, Giroux (1980) states CE curricula that fall under a hermeneutic rationality stress "negotiation, participation and the importance of values in CE" (p. 342) and place a strong emphasis on "social construction rather than the imposed nature of the classroom" (p. 343), which provide meaningful interactions with the meaning and purpose of CE. Such an approach transcends models of citizenship transmission and can promote pluralistic definitions of citizenship. However, while CE curricula established within a hermeneutic rationality accommodate subjective and relativistic forms of knowledge, Giroux (1980) asserts it is exactly these notions of knowledge that weaken its epistemological foundation by not providing opportunities for historical analysis or platforms for critique: Thus, by reducing power and democratic action to the level of an epistemology that supports forms of subjective idealism, the reflective inquiry approach emerges as a one-sided theory of CE which has "miraculously" abstracted its social epistemology from such troublesome concepts as ideology, power, struggle, and oppression (p. 343).

In short, hermeneutic rationale rejects objectivism, but it fails to develop an analysis that leads to "an open, self-critical community of inquiring citizens" (Giroux 1980, p. 346). In both modes of rationality, the socialisation of pupils to dominant ideologies and normative values is enhanced by a form of schooling established on epistemological positions that do not accommodate or promote "negotiated outcomes and critical thinking" (Giroux 1980, p. 345). Emancipatory rationality attempts to address hermeneutic interests in order to explore how such interests place "specific limitations and constraints upon human thought and action" (Giroux 1980, p. 346). This process is established upon the principles of critique and praxis. In other words, emancipatory rationality informs critical reflection and knowledge construction and is concerned with demystifying ideology that prevents a critique of the "political, social and economic contradictions" (Freire 2000, p. 35) that exist in our daily lives. Giroux further discusses two educational traditions informed by an emancipatory rationality: political economy and culturalist positions. The political economy position is oriented to how macrostructural relationships organise and reproduce class relations. Culturalists are oriented to the "experiences of subjects and how notions of consciousness, ideology and power enter into the way human beings constitute their day-to-day lives" (Giroux 1980 p. 348). The underlying assumption of emancipatory rationality that informs these positions puts forward the process of social reproduction as the primary organising factor for schooling. In other words, schooling acts as a mediator between pupils and their social relations, orienting them to regard the dominancy of certain groups and structures as naturally occurring components of social life (Apple 2004; Bernstein 2003; Bourdieu and Passeron 1990).

As mentioned above, the Curriculum Cymreig is situated within a cultural citizenship framework that promotes an understanding of citizenship as a cultural association derived from essentially Welsh characteristics such as language use and bloodline. Such an approach fits well into a theory of social and cultural reproduction in that it operationalises a technical rationale in promoting and normalising discourses of Welshness as an objective characteristic—a naturally occurring, a priori position suggesting a "true" or "innate" Welshness inhabiting various positions of power that infuse social structures and inform traditional practices. From these negotiations of power and position, derivative forms of Welshness are generated and organised into hierarchies of Welshness experienced by pupils, with pupils who inhabit non-regular orientations to dominate discourses of Welshness experiencing greater levels of disassociation with Welshness and Wales. It is possible that the variations in the data presented here are an indicator of such reproductions.

For example, pupils having non-white ethnic backgrounds regularly express negative interpretations of school's impact on their associations with Wales, while white pupils and pupils fluent in the Welsh language report the opposite. For each of the Curriculum Cymreig statements, Year 8 pupils agreed more often than Year 10 pupils. Perhaps, in addition to the points raised earlier, this is a result of pupils naively participating in a curriculum that does not accommodate critical enquiry and reflection, which is not a surprise since these pupils attend schools in which teachers are not prepared to encourage and facilitate discussions of culture and inclusion (Philpott and Dagenais 2011; Rapoport 2010). The technical rationale organising the Curriculum Cymreig offers an objective form of Welshness that pupils who have not yet developed robust forms of critique accept as a "complete story," a commonsensical representation of Wales and Welshness that is both simple and natural. The Curriculum Cymreig is promoted as a constructivist curriculum (Smith 2010) in that it claims to provide pupils opportunities to engage in learning experiences intended to help them develop their own sense of Welshness and social interaction within their communities. While, as part of a larger discussion of citizenship and community, it is concerned with how pupils in Wales are introduced to discussions of civic life and democratic living, as a curricular initiative its theoretical foundations do not allow for pupils to consider the social, political, and economic factors that intersect and shape orientations to cultural identity and citizenship. Giroux (1980) stresses that the governance of individuals' socialisation is managed through macro-level economic and political structures, and that through acquiring an awareness of the nature of such governance and "the potential for acting upon it" (p. 347), individuals can perceive the factors organising their orientation to the world, formulate more socially just and inclusive alternatives, and bring about change informed from those critically informed reflective processes. With the implementation of CE in schools comes the necessity for educators and policymakers to incorporate more distinct, child-oriented forms of democracy and democratic education (Koshmanova 2006; Maitles and Deuchar 2006). If CE in Wales is to include a curricular initiative designed to promote Welshness and celebrate the diversity of life in Wales, it should also include opportunities for teachers and pupils to critically engage in dialectical discussions of identity, self, and other—including discussions about nationalism rather than simply learning activities that promote it (McDonough and Andrée-Anne 2013) as well as the social, political, and economic forces that orientate pupils' perspectives on citizenship and participation in the public sphere.

REFERENCES

Andrews, R., & Lewis, G. (2000). Citizenship education in Wales: Community, culture and the Curriculum Cymreig. http://www.leeds.ac.uk/educol/documents/00001571.htm

Apple, M. (2004). *Ideology and curriculum*. London: Routledge.
Apple, M. W. (2008). Can schooling contribute to a more just society? *Education, Citizenship and Social Justice, 3*(3), 239–261.
Aronowitz, S., & Giroux, H. A. (1993). *Education still under Siege* (2nd ed.). Westport: Bergin & Garvey.
Bates, R. (2006). Educational administration and social justice. *Education, Citizenship and Social Justice, 1*(2), 141–156.
Bernstein, B. (2003). *Towards a theory of educational transmission* (3rd ed.). New York: Routledge.
Bourdieu, P., & Passeron, J. (1990). *Cultural reproduction and social reproduction* (2nd ed.). Thousand Oaks: Sage.
Brubaker, R., & Cooper, F. (2000). Beyond identity. *Theory and Society, 29*, 1–47.
Freire, P. (1985). *The politics of education: Culture, power and liberation*. South Hadley: Bergin & Garvey.
Freire, P. (2000). *Pedagogy of the oppressed* (30th Anniversary edition). New York: The Continuum International Publishing Group.
Freire, P. (2006). *Pedagogy of the oppressed* (30th Anniversary edition). New York: The Continuum International Publishing Group.
Gillborn, D. (2006). Citizenship education as placebo: 'Standards', institutional racism and education policy. *Education, Citizenship and Social Justice, 1*(1), 83–104.
Giroux, H. A. (1980). Critical theory and rationality in citizenship education. *Curriculum Inquiry, 10*(4), 329–366.
Giroux, H. A. (1981). *Ideology, culture and the process of schooling*. Philadelphia/London: Temple University Press/Falmer Press.
Giroux, H. A. (2010a). In defense of public school teachers in a time of crisis. *Policy Futures in Education, 8*(6), 709–714.
Giroux, H. A. (2010b). Rethinking education as the practice of freedom: Paulo Freire and the promise of critical pedagogy. *Policy Futures in Education, 8*(6), 715–721.
Giroux, H. A. (2011). *On critical pedagogy*. New York: The Continuum International Publishing Group.
Giroux, H. A. (2012). *Education and the crisis of public values: Challenging the assault on teachers, students, and public education*. New York: Peter Lang.
Koshmanova, T. (2006). National identity and cultural coherence in educational reform for democratic citizenship: The case of Ukraine. *Education, Citizenship and Social Justice, 1*(1), 105–118.
Macey, D. (2001). *Dictionary of critical theory*. London: Penguin.
Maitles, H., & Deuchar, R. (2006). 'We don't learn democracy, we live it!': Consulting the pupil voice in Scottish schools. *Education, Citizenship and Social Justice, 1*(3), 249–266.

McDonough, K., & Andrée-Anne, C. (2013). Beyond patriotic education: Locating the place of nationalism in the public school curriculum. *Education, Citizenship and Social Justice, 8*(2), 135–150.

Philpott, R., & Dagenais, D. (2011). Grappling with social justice: Exploring new teachers' practice and experiences. *Education, Citizenship and Social Justice, 7*(1), 85–99.

Rapoport, A. (2010). We cannot teach what we don't know: Indiana teachers talk about global citizenship education. *Education, Citizenship and Social Justice, 5*(3), 179–190.

Sleeter, C., & Grant, C. (2003). *Making choices for multicultural education: Five approaches to race, class, and gender* (4th ed.). New York: Wiley.

Smith, K. J. (2010). A critical discourse analysis of developing the curriculum Cymreig the language of learning Welshness. http://rave.ohiolink.edu/etdc/view?acc%5Fnum=miami1292251849

Smith, K. (2015). Fy ardal/my neighbourhood: How might pupils' orientations to their neighbourhood contribute to a pedagogy of place? *Environmental Education Research.* doi:10.1080/13504622.2015.1118747.

Welsh Government. (2003). Developing the Curriculum Cymreig. Retrieved August 13, 2015 from http://learning.gov.wales/docs/learningwales/publications/130424-developing-the-curriculum-cymreig-en.pdf

BIBLIOGRAPHY

Furlong, J., & Phillips, R. (2001). *Education, reform and the state: Twenty five years of politics, policy and practice*. London: Routledge.

Government of Wales Act. (2006). Retrieved November 25, 2008 from http://wales.gov.uk/about/?lang=en

Phillips, R., & Daughtery, R. (2001). Educational devolution and nation building in Wales: A different 'Great Debate'? In R. Phillips & J. Furlong (Eds.), *Education reform and the state: Twenty-five years of politics, policy and practice*. London: Routledge.

Welsh Language Act 1993. (1993). Retrieved September 7, 2015 from http://www.legislation.gov.uk/ukpga/1993/38/contents

© The Editor(s) (if applicable) and The Author(s) 2016   101
K. Smith, *Curriculum, Culture and Citizenship Education in Wales*,
DOI 10.1057/978-1-137-54443-8

INDEX

philosophical framework of, 90
policy by primary and secondary
    schools, 64
in primary schools, 87
and pupils, 59–64
revisiting, in school, 66–9
in secondary schools, 46, 90
teaching Welshness, 72–5
curriculum development
and educational policy, 37
and implementation, 42
in Wales, 19
Cymraeg, 14, 29, 48–50, 52, 62, 88
reclamation of, 21
recognition of, 36
in schools, 19–21
as Welshness, 53–4

D
democratic disaffectedness, 2
denomination
religious, 16–17
Welsh Calvinistic Methodist, 24
Developing the Curriculum Cymreig,
    38, 59, 60, 73, 78, 83, 94
citizenship and cultural identity, 5
critical discourse analysis of, 45–8
Phillips, 4
Welsh Government, 4, 43, 45, 91
Welshness in, 82
devolutionary powers, 11, 12
Dewey, 30
Dury, 18

E
education. *See also* citizenship
    education (CE); Welsh education
contemporary, 20, 21, 42, 91
formal, 14–16, 18
transformational power of, 25

Education Act of 2002, 7
educational history of Wales, 11–14
and medieval ages, 14–15
rebellion, reformation, and
    renaissance, 15–19
educational leaders, 13
educational philanthropy, 31
educational policy, 2, 14, 20, 70
curriculum development and, 37
development of, 31, 37
Welsh, 62
educational policymakers, 2
educational reform, 35
Education for Sustainable
    Development and Global
    Citizenship (ESDGC), 2
culture and cultural identity frame
    by, 8
development and sustainability of,
    6–7
guidance for, 83–4
implementation of, 5, 6
inspections of, 5
policies and practice, 6
presence and effectiveness of school,
    5–6
programme, 7
supplementary guidance for, 5
teaching and learning in, 6
in Welsh Baccalaureate curriculum,
    6
Education Reform Act of 1988, 37, 42
educators, 4, 5, 7, 21, 28, 30, 40–1,
    45, 78
and policymakers, 2, 98
Swedish theologian and, 18
in Wales, 40
Edwards, Owen, 29, 37, 38, 40
Chief Inspector of Education for
    Wales, 29, 30
Dewey's work, 30
Elizabeth, Queen, 18

educational philanthropy in, 31
educational policy development in,
37
educators in, 40
English imperialism in, 12, 14, 28
formal education of, 18
future of colonisation in, 12
National Assembly for Wales, 12
national curriculum for, 4, 37, 40,
42
new intermediate schools in, 30
public education in, 27
rebellion, 16
secondary schools, 48
Welsh culture in schools in, 30,
36–7
Welsh population in, 21
Webster, Noah, 41
Welsh Assembly Government's
document Rights to Action, 7
Welsh Baccalaureate, 2, 6, 69, 71, 72,
76–7, 92
Welsh Bible, 22
Welsh Calvinistic Methodist
denomination, 24
Welsh clergy, 17
Welsh cultural identity, 79, 92
Welsh culture, 29, 88
historical and cultural aspects
of, 79
in schools in Wales, 30, 36–7
Welsh curricular policy, 9
Welsh curriculum authority, 36
Welsh Department of Education,
29–30
Welsh education, 12–14
and culture, 21
distinctive feature of, 88
domain of, 26
flagship policies of, 69
history of, 28

inadequacies of, 27
policy, 62
theoretical paradigm in, 40
Welsh government, 5, 78, 80
Community and Understanding, 3–4
Developing the Curriculum Cymreig,
4, 43, 45, 91
devolution of, 35–6
PSE Framework by, 7, 8
Welsh identity, 13, 38, 46
Welsh language, 22, 48, 62, 64, 87
consensual attack on, 20
institutionalisation of prejudice
against, 20
recognisation, 21
in teaching, 24
Welsh Language Act of 1993, 21
Welsh language policy, 74, 88
Welshness
beyond, 81–6
citizenship and, 70, 92
cultural identity and, 75–8
curricularising, 86–9
Cymraeg as, 53–4
derivative forms of, 97
in *Developing the Curriculum
Cymreig*, 82
discursive formations of, 86
distinctiveness of Wales and, 46
and ethnicity, 88
family and community
traditions, 54
learning, 58–69
learning experiences and, 56–8
locating, 89–91
management of, 46
method of identification and
association with, 46
sense of, 46, 47, 74, 84, 85
students' perceptions of, 48–54
teaching, 69–78